IERI Monograph Series

Issues and Methodologies in Large-Scale Assessments

VOLUME 4

IERI

IEA **ETS.**

October 2011

ISBN 978-088685411-9

Copies of this publication can be obtained from:

IERInstitute
IEA Data Processing and Research Center
Mexikoring 37
22297 Hamburg,
Germany

IERInstitute
Educational Testing Service
Mail Stop 02-R
Princeton, NJ 08541,
United States

By email: ierinstitute@iea-dpc.de
Free downloads: www.ierinstitute.org

Copyeditors: Paula Wagemaker, Editorial Services, Christchurch, New Zealand with David Robitaille, and Ruth R. Greenwood
Design and production by Becky Bliss Design and Production, Wellington, New Zealand

IERI Monograph Series

Issues and Methodologies in Large-Scale Assessments

Volume 4	2011

TABLE OF CONTENTS

Introduction

Matthias von Davier (Editor)
Educational Testing Service

Dirk Hastedt (Editor)
IEA Data Processing and Research Center

For more than four years, the International Association for the Evaluation of Educational Achievement (IEA) and Educational Testing Service (ETS) have worked together in the IEA-ETS Research Institute (IERI). IERI undertakes activities focused on three broad areas of work: research studies related to the development and implementation of large-scale assessments of educational outcomes, professional development and training, and dissemination of research findings and information gathered through large-scale assessments. Part of IEA and ETS's collaborative work focuses on improving the science of large-scale assessments.

In this fourth volume of our periodical, we have collected a number of what we consider are very interesting papers that contribute to discussion about the analysis and findings of such assessments. Each paper has in common its authors' efforts to deal with very specific and applied problems of analyzing international large-scale assessment data. Two of the papers use the IEA Progress in Reading Literacy Study (PIRLS) data, one uses the IEA Trends in International Mathematics and Science Study (TIMSS) data, two more employ OECD Programme for International Student Achievement (PISA) data, and the remaining paper employs IEA Teacher Education and Development Study in Mathematics (TEDS-M) data. All six papers contribute to discussions on methods used to analyze large-scale assessment data by critically reviewing the designs and analyses of these surveys and their data.

In the first paper, *Age Distribution and Reading Achievement Configurations among Fourth-Grade Students in PIRLS 2006*, authors Michael Martin, Ina Mullis, and Pierre Foy use PIRLS 2006 reading achievement results for fourth-grade students in 36 countries for their analyses. They show how variations in countries' policies on age of school entry and on promotion and retention make it difficult to determine a straightforward relationship between age within grade and achievement across countries. Although, in some countries, older fourth-grade students have higher achievement than younger students, older students do not necessarily perform better. The paper presents an interesting application of a regression discontinuity technique that the authors performed on data from countries with a strict cut-off for student progression from grade to grade.

The second paper, *The Influences of Home Language, Gender, and Social Class on Mathematics Literacy in France, Germany, Hong Kong, and the United States*, authors Aminah Perkins, Laura Quaynor, and George Engelhard, Jr. used data from four countries in order to analyze the relationships between home language, gender, and social class, and mathematics literacy. The data used came from PISA 2003. The authors used Rasch measurement and applied a clever approach wherein item difficulties were fixed to the operational valued from PISA. They also paid special attention to person response functions within the context of their analyses. The authors concluded that there are important differences between the groups under study. They suggested that their analyses should be replicated with data from more recent PISA cycles, and that this work should employ more recent estimation techniques and involve a larger group of participating countries.

In the third paper, *Hierarchical Factor Item Response Theory Models for PIRLS: Capturing Clustering Effects at Multiple Levels*, author Frank Rijmen presents a sophisticated analysis of data from an international large-scale assessment. He shows how modern psychometric methodologies can be applied to even large data-sets with a complex linking structure across test forms as well as complex dependencies between items due to the passage structure of the reading assessment. The use of forward-looking methodologies, such as the one that Rijmen presents, is becoming ever more important in terms of aiding our understanding of increasingly complex assessments that employ technology and more authentic item formats.

Diagnostic Cluster Analysis of Mathematics Skills, the fourth paper, is written by Yoon Soo Park and Young-Sun Lee and draws on TIMSS 2007 fourth-grade mathematics data. The authors present an alternative means of gaining a better understanding of how different skill domains are related across countries. The authors do not apply clustering to achieve classification of individuals. Instead, they classify skills into more homogeneous groups with respect to country selection. This process requires assigning each item the number of skills that are required to solve the item. When doing this, the authors drew on substantive support from content experts, such that they were able to provide the clustering solution for the required skills into more homogeneous clusters of skills for a number of countries.

The fifth paper, *TEDS-M: Diagnosing Teacher Knowledge by Applying Multidimensional Item Response Theory and Multiple-Group Models*, by Sigrid Blömeke, Richard Houang, and Ute Suhl, presents an analysis of TEDS-M data. The authors conducted this analysis in order to compare different multidimensional Rasch-type IRT models and to consider their utility in establishing latent variables suitable for representing teachers' pedagogical content knowledge. The authors also address the question of population invariance and how the multidimensional models applied can help to inform research with respect to this issue.

PISA Test Format Assessment and the Local Independence Assumption, the sixth paper, by Christian Monseur, Ariane Baye, Dominique Lafontaine, and Valérie Quittre, provides an interesting application of measures that could be called, following Molenaar (1983), fit diagnostics. The authors explore whether local dependency is an issue in international large-scale assessments and whether taking the dependencies into account may allow us to better understand the results of these assessments.

We hope you will find reading these papers as interesting as we did. We also hope that you will consider supporting this periodical by submitting your own methodological research on international large-scale assessments to IERI.

Reference

Molenaar, I. W. (1983). Some improved diagnostics for failure in the Rasch model. *Psychometrics*, *48*, 49–75.

About IEA

The International Association for the Evaluation of Educational Achievement (IEA) is an independent, non-profit, international cooperative of national research institutions and governmental research agencies. Through its comparative research and assessment projects, IEA aims to:

- Provide international benchmarks that can assist policymakers to identify the comparative strengths and weaknesses of their education systems;
- Provide high-quality data that will increase policymakers' understanding of key school-based and non-school-based factors that influence teaching and learning;
- Provide high-quality data that will serve as a resource for identifying areas of concern and action, and for preparing and evaluating educational reforms;
- Develop and improve the capacity of educational systems to engage in national strategies for educational monitoring and improvement; and
- Contribute to development of the worldwide community of researchers in educational evaluation.

Additional information about IEA is available at www.iea.nl and www.iea-dpc.de.

About ETS

ETS is a non-profit institution whose mission is to advance quality and equity in education by providing fair and valid assessments, research, and related services for all people worldwide. In serving individuals, educational institutions, and government agencies around the world, ETS customizes solutions to meet the need for teacher professional development products and services, classroom and end-of-course assessments, and research-based teaching and learning tools. Founded in 1947, ETS today develops, administers, and scores more than 24 million tests annually in more than 180 countries, at over 9,000 locations worldwide.

Additional information about ETS is available at www.ets.org.

Age distribution and reading achievement configurations among fourth-grade students in PIRLS 2006

An analysis of the German 2006 PIRLS data

Michael O. Martin, Ina V. S. Mullis, and Pierre Foy
TIMSS & PIRLS International Study Center, Boston College, Chestnut Hill, Massachusetts, USA

This study used the Progress in International Reading Literacy Study (PIRLS) 2006 reading achievement results for fourth-grade students in 36 countries to show how variations in countries' policies on age of school entry and promotion and retention make it difficult to determine a straightforward relationship between age-within-grade and achievement across countries. Although, in some countries, older Grade 4 students had higher achievement than younger students, older students did not necessarily perform better. Many countries had a substantial proportion of older students in the fourth grade (students whose age suggests they belong in a higher grade), and these older students had significantly lower achievement than their younger classmates. The different configurations of age-within-grade across countries make it problematic to statistically adjust countries' average reading achievement for differences in age. Thus, comparisons across countries in how chronological age and amount of schooling influence achievement must be made with care.

IERI Monograph Series: Issues and Methodologies in Large-Scale Assessments Volume 4

INTRODUCTION

The International Association for the Evaluation of Educational Achievement (IEA)'s assessment of student achievement in mathematics and science (TIMSS) and assessment of reading achievement (PIRLS) are grade-based assessments, which means that the target population is all the students at a particular grade level—four and eight for TIMSS and four for PIRLS. IEA's focus on grade as the basis for its target populations contrasts with the Organisation for Economic Co-operation and Development (OECD)'s Programme for International Student Assessment (PISA) survey, which assesses mathematics literacy, science literacy, and reading literacy among 15-year-olds (OECD, 2001).

IEA considers that, for its major purpose of improving educational achievement, amount of schooling provides a more useful basis than age for interpreting and using the results of international comparisons. Although the PISA approach of assessing students by age provides an absolutely clear basis for defining the samples of students to be assessed, TIMSS and PIRLS assess student achievement by grade because this maximizes the opportunity to link educational achievement to policies, curriculum, and instructional practices. Since most educational initiatives are implemented at particular grade levels, TIMSS and PIRLS data can readily be used as a basis for implementing and monitoring educational reform and improving student achievement. Also, because mathematics, science, and (perhaps to a lesser extent) reading are curriculum dependent and learned largely in school, IEA views amount of instruction as the major determinant of educational achievement.

A number of studies during the past several decades have investigated the effects of chronological age and amount of schooling on achievement, with most showing that the effects of schooling are greater than the effects of age. For example, Cliffordson and Gustafsson (2007) used regression analyses of simultaneous variation in age and length of schooling to investigate the effects of age and amount of schooling on Swedish military enlistees' test scores. After reviewing the enlistment scores of an entire cohort of 18-year-old males, the authors concluded that both age and schooling increased performance on two aspects of student ability—crystallized intelligence and general visualization—and that the effects of amount of schooling were considerably stronger than the effects of age.

Recently, interest in using TIMSS and PIRLS data to research the effects of age and amount of schooling has increased. However, using grade (determined by years of formal schooling) as the basis for comparison makes variation in the age of the students an important consideration. We discuss, in the next section, several attempts to model variation in age or to adjust for it, but caution that if analytical approaches such as these are to be more widely used, there needs to be a clear understanding of how policies and practices influencing assignment to grade relate to age and how this association varies from country to country. Within a single grade level, the TIMSS and PIRLS demographic data show that average student age can vary across countries by as much as one year (Mullis, Martin, Foy, et al., 2008; Mullis, Martin,

Kennedy, & Foy, 2007). In general, this is because students' age of entry to primary school varies (typically, children enter school at six to seven years of age), and because promotion and retention policies also vary. Also, the practices of parents can be flexible; sometimes they accord with the formal policies and sometimes not. Because it is difficult to assemble information describing variations in patterns of age-within-grade across countries as well as providing explanations for the differences, such information unfortunately is not readily available.

The central purpose of this paper is to describe the distribution of student age within the fourth grade in the countries that participated in PIRLS 2006 and to examine how that distribution related to achievement. We used the PIRLS 2006 international database (Foy & Kennedy, 2008) containing reading achievement results for fourth-grade students in 40 countries[1] in this study in order to examine the distributions of fourth-graders by birth month. We considered age distributions in the light of the participating countries' reports of their policies and practices regarding ages of entry to primary school and policies on promotion and retention.[2] We augmented this information with more recent material from the *TIMSS 2007 Encyclopedia* (Mullis, Martin, Olson, et al., 2008). Finally, we looked at the relationships between various patterns of distribution by birth month and reading achievement in several of the PIRLS 2006 countries.

RESEARCH USING INTERNATIONAL DATA TO INVESTIGATE THE EFFECTS OF AGE AND AMOUNT OF SCHOOLING

In one notable attempt to examine the interrelationships among age, grade, and achievement, Luyten (2006) applied a regression discontinuity approach in a multilevel modeling context using data from TIMSS 1995. The regression discontinuity approach is a quasi-experimental analytic technique that can be applied to achievement data from adjacent grades to estimate the effect of schooling.[3] Luyten explained that this approach, sometimes referred to as a cutting-point design, had been applied previously to estimate the independent effects of age and schooling on achievement in a 1973 study of primary education in Israel. In the initial study, Cahan and Cohen (1989) found that the effect of one year of schooling was substantial, having as much as twice the effect of one year of age.

The drawback of the regression discontinuity approach is that it requires achievement data from countries where admission to school depends primarily on a student's date of birth. If the country has a strict policy of admitting students to school on a particular date when they are at a particular age (e.g., all children who have turned six by January 1), the data from two consecutive grades can be used to assess the absolute

---

1 As described in a later section, this paper is restricted to data from 36 countries, with the Flemish and French parts of Belgium seen as separate entities.

2 These reports were assembled in the *PIRLS 2006 Encyclopedia* (Kennedy, Mullis, Martin, & Trong, 2007).

3 The present paper includes an application of the regression discontinuity design to data from two countries, Iceland and Norway, both of which participated in PIRLS 2006 with two adjacent grades.

contribution of schooling to students' achievement. While the regular increase in age by birth month for the students can be related to achievement for each grade, we can anticipate a discontinuity between the oldest students in the lower grade and the youngest students in the higher grade. That is, the students beginning the next higher grade will be not be much older (born in January rather than in the previous December), but they will have had one more year of school. Based on the 26 countries participating in TIMSS 1995 at the primary-school level, Luyten (2006) found eight countries that met his criteria of having a sharp cutoff date, namely, Cyprus, Greece, England, Iceland, Japan, Norway, Scotland, and Singapore. The analysis of the TIMSS 1995 mathematics and science data from Grades 3 and 4 in these countries showed strong schooling effects on achievement.

In another attempt to control for age, Luyten, Peschar, and Coe (2008) used data from PISA 2000 to analyze the effects of age and schooling on the reading literacy of 15-year-olds in England. Capitalizing on the fact that children in England begin school strictly in accordance with their date of birth and that approximately half the national sample of 15-year-olds was in Grade 10 and half in Grade 11, these authors employed a regression discontinuity approach within a multilevel modeling framework to examine the effect of an extra grade of schooling while controlling for students' age. Luyten and his colleagues found a modest positive effect of schooling on reading performance, even though the PISA reading assessment was not designed to reflect a specific school curriculum. Also, we might expect that students typically would have mastered their reading skills by Grade 10 and thus have less room for growth than would have been the case earlier in their schooling careers. Yet, the authors noted, only one third of the extra grade effect could be accounted for by age differences, a finding which implies that "most of the advantage for the students in the upper grade must be due to the effect of schooling" (Luyten et al., 2008, p. 336).

Recognizing that policies on age of school entry and promotion and retention result in variation in student age, Cliffordson (2008) also employed a between-grade regression discontinuity design to analyze TIMSS 1995 data from Sweden; her focus was on Grades 6, 7, and 8. Although this design provides a powerful technique for analyzing adjacent grade data, such as those in TIMSS 1995, the author acknowledged that when the design is used to separate the effects of age and grade, it "relies on the assumptions that there is a sharp age-based decision rule for grade assignment, and that the regression of performance on age is linear" (p. 3). Accordingly, one of Cliffordson's major purposes for conducting the study was to assess the extent to which these assumptions were tenable for the Swedish TIMSS data. Cliffordson's results for her analyses comparing the achievement of sixth- and seventh-grade students in mathematics and science were broadly in line with the studies described above, with the effect of schooling about twice as strong as the effect of age. Analyses based on the data for the seventh- and eighth-grade students showed a weaker schooling effect, particularly for science, although it was still stronger than the age effect.

Cliffordson's (2008) analyses also revealed that the bias in estimating age and school effects due to departures from a sharp age-based decision rule for grade assignment was relatively small in the Swedish data. However, she noted that this outcome was probably because the percentage of "normal-aged" students (students in the appropriate grade for their age) was very high in the Swedish sample. Departures from the grade assignment rule affected only about 3.5% of students, and so the potential for bias was limited. She cautioned that her results did not imply that bias would remain low if the proportion of students not of normal age for their cohort was excessive.

The studies described above show that it is possible to use quasi-experimental techniques such as regression discontinuity analysis with adjacent grade data to estimate the effect of age-within-grade on student achievement, provided that students are assigned to grades solely on the basis of age and that no other factors related to achievement are involved. For example, Van Damme, Vanhee, and Pustjens (2008), generalizing from previous work, statistically adjusted average reading achievement to control for differences in average age among the countries that participated in PIRLS 2006. They applied the same correction factor to all countries, regardless of the relationship between age and reading achievement evident in each. However, it is fundamental to recognize that students' age-within-grade can be manipulated by policy decisions and, in particular, that policies on age of entry to school and policies on promotion/retention can influence not just the average age but also the age distribution within a grade.

Conscious of the need for an analytic approach to estimating the effects of schooling that makes less restrictive assumptions about the role of age, Luyten and Veldkamp (2008) applied a two-step procedure suggested by Heckman (1979) to reanalyze the TIMSS 1995 data for Grades 3 and 4. This procedure, as a first step, explicitly models the role of age in assigning students to a grade and then, as a second step, includes a correction factor derived from the model in a regression equation. The intention behind including the correction factor is to control for any selection bias caused by factors other than age influencing the grade assignment process.

Luyten and Veldkamp (2008) found it possible to model the grade-assignment process adequately in 15 of the 26 countries that participated in TIMSS 1995 at the primary level, and to apply the Heckman procedure successfully in these countries. On average, across the countries, the authors estimated that schooling accounted for 51% of the mathematics achievement difference between third and fourth grades and for 45% of the science difference. The effect sizes varied widely across countries, from 29% in England to 72% in the Netherlands for mathematics and from 14% in Canada to 69% in Korea for science.

Both Cliffordson (2008) and Luyten and Veldkamp (2008) acknowledged, when reporting the results of their studies, that anyone wanting to use adjacent grades to estimate the effect of schooling across countries needs to understand how students' ages are used to assign students to grades. Taking the above methodology a step further, Cliffordson and Gustafsson (2010) reanalyzed the Swedish TIMSS 1995 data using an instrumental variables regression approach that relaxed the assumption that there is a sharp age-based decision rule for grade assignment. Finding the results for this one country encouraging, the authors recommended that the method be further investigated with data from other countries. However, because the instrumental variables approach is also based on creating an instrumental variable that adequately models the age–grade assignment process, it too requires an understanding of how policies and practice with regard to age of entry to school and grade promotion/retention influence the distribution of age-within-grade.

Because the 40 countries that participated in PIRLS 2006 represented a wide range of policy approaches, we considered that an analysis of the age distribution within grade in terms of the different entry and promotion and retention policies of these countries could be used to investigate the relationship between these policies and the distribution of students' age-within-grade. Educational researchers can use this information to inform attempts to model the grade assignment process more effectively, while educational decisionmakers can use it to understand the effects on achievement of students starting school at younger or older ages, as well as the likely effects on achievement of various promotion and retention policies.

DISTRIBUTION OF STUDENT AGES IN THE PIRLS 2006 TARGET GRADE

As described in the *PIRLS 2006 Encyclopedia* (Kennedy et al., 2007), countries' admission policies generally require children to begin primary school when they are six or seven years old. As already discussed, a number of the studies about the effects of age and schooling on achievement have used the regression discontinuity model, which requires data from a country with a strict adherence to a nationwide cutoff point that determines if a student is in a higher or a lower grade. If we assume a uniform birth rate across the months of a year,[4] an age-of-entry policy based on students' dates of birth would result in an approximately equal proportion of students in each birth month. Thus, a full cohort of students would contain approximately equal percentages of students born in January, February, March, and so on. Because there are 12 months in a year, approximately eight percent of students would be evident in each birth month. We could expect to see this pattern in countries with strict policies on age of entry and automatic promotion from grade to grade.

How countries implement policies about age of entry into school varies from country to country, thereby contributing to the variety of age distributions across those countries. Countries with more flexible practices with respect to age of entry can have different age distributions within a grade, as can countries with promotion policies based on examination results, or retention or acceleration practices based on school or teacher recommendations.

---

4   Although the odds of being born in a particular month vary somewhat across the 12 months of the year, fluctuations from month to month are relatively small and the odds are sufficiently uniform for the purposes of this argument.

Figure 1 shows the distribution of students' ages, on average, as well as by birth month across the PIRLS 2006 countries that assessed students in their fourth year of formal schooling and that collected data according to the Northern Hemisphere schedule of April to May, 2005.[5] The figure presents the countries in decreasing order by predominant age cohort; countries where students were older, on average, are at the top of the figure, and those where students were younger are at the bottom. The bar chart accompanying each country depicts the percentage of students at each month of birth; the 12 adjacent months that include the greatest percentage of students are highlighted to identify the predominant age cohort for the grade (i.e., the 12 adjacent months that define the greatest percentage of students). This approach not only groups countries with similar age distributions but also shows the cumulative effects of school admission policies and promotion and retention practices through the grades on the distribution of student ages at the fourth grade. In general, few countries had all of their students within this 12-month interval; most had more widespread distributions, in some cases spanning several years.

The countries in the first grouping in Figure 1 require students to begin primary school in the calendar year in which they turn seven. Thus, the students assessed in PIRLS 2006 predominantly were born in the 1995 calendar year. The countries included in this first group were Denmark, Bulgaria, Latvia, Lithuania, Moldova, Romania, the Russian Federation, and Sweden. Students in these countries were among the oldest in the PIRLS 2006 assessment—approximately 10.8 years of age, on average.

Among this group of countries, Sweden was the country where the predominant age cohort included practically all students at fourth grade; there were very few younger or older students. This pattern indicates a relatively strict adherence to the nationwide cutoff dates, as discussed by the researchers who used the Swedish data from TIMSS 1995 (see above). Also, Sweden has a policy of automatic promotion from grade to grade. However, the other countries in this group had noticeable percentages of older and, in some cases, younger students. Among these, Latvia, Lithuania, Romania, and the Russian Federation reported that promotion from grade to grade depended on students' progress; retention was thus a contributing factor to having older students.

The set of countries in Figure 1 in which the predominant cohort was born in 1995 is followed by several countries where the predominant cohort was not confined to a single calendar year but spanned two years. In Hungary, where children normally should be six years old by May 31 in order to begin school in September, the predominant cohort extended from March 1995 through February 1996, as also was the case for Macedonia. Both countries also had substantial percentages of older and younger students in the fourth grade, although only Hungary reported basing its promotion policy on students' progress.

---

5 PIRLS 2006 also included two countries that tested at Grade 5 (South Africa and Luxembourg), three countries where the school year is conducted on a Southern Hemisphere schedule (Singapore and New Zealand, in addition to South Africa), and five Canadian provinces. However, to simplify the basis for comparing age distributions across countries, we have not included these participants in Figures 1, 2, and 3.

Figure 1: PIRLS 2006 percentage of students by month of birth

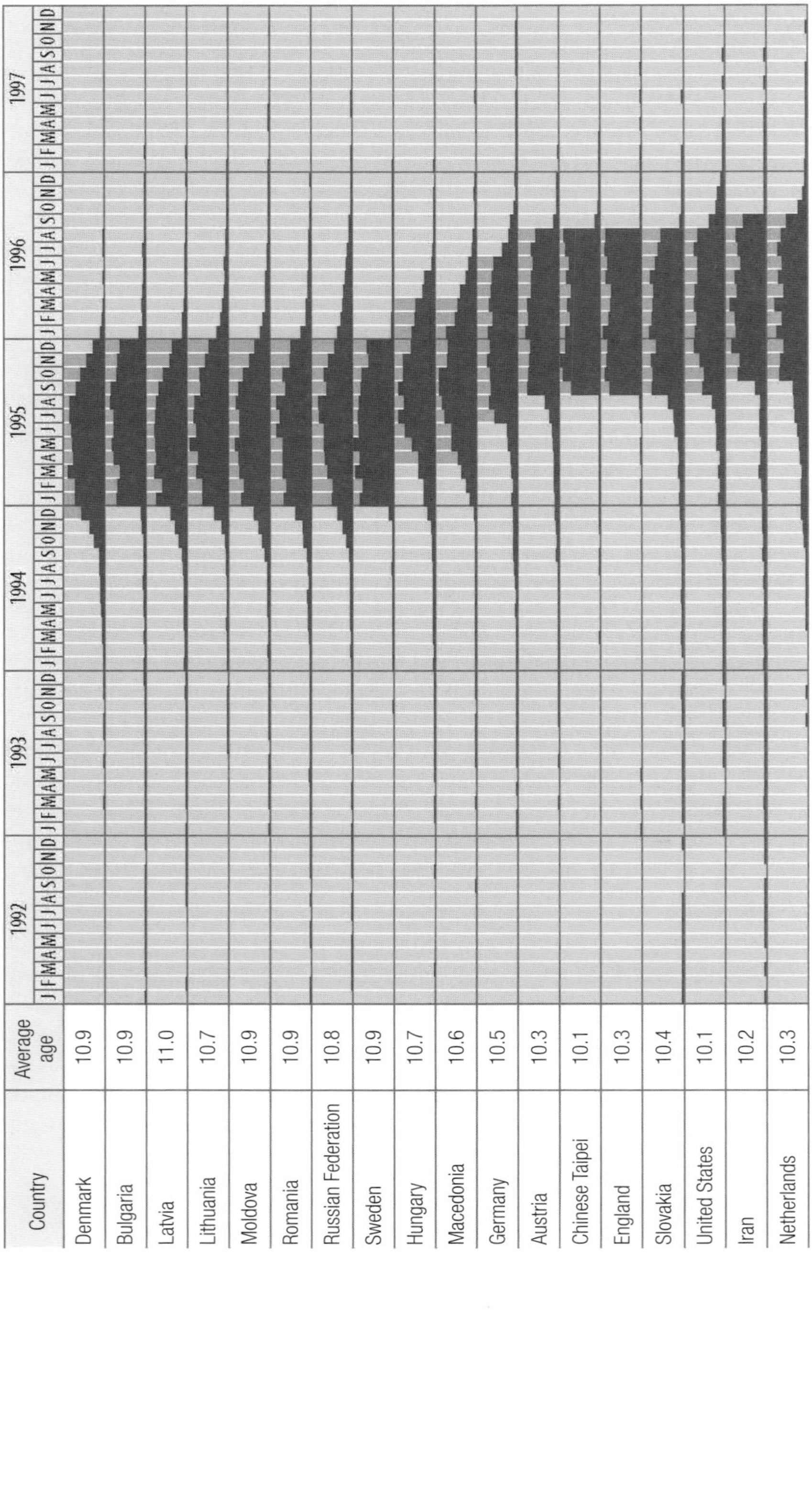
Country
Average age
1992
1993
1994
1995
1996
1997
J F M A M J J A S O N D
Denmark 10.9
Bulgaria 10.9
Latvia 11.0
Lithuania 10.7
Moldova 10.9
Romania 10.9
Russian Federation 10.8
Sweden 10.9
Hungary 10.7
Macedonia 10.6
Germany 10.5
Austria 10.3
Chinese Taipei 10.1
England 10.3
Slovakia 10.4
United States 10.1
Iran 10.2
Netherlands 10.3

Figure 1: PIRLS 2006 percentage of students by month of birth (Contd.)

Country	Average age
Georgia	10.1
Indonesia	10.4
Israel	10.1
Belgium (Flemish)	10.0
Belgium (French)	9.9
France	10.0
Hong Kong (SAR)	10.0
Iceland	9.8
Italy	9.7
Morocco	10.8
Norway	9.8
Poland	9.9
Slovenia	9.9
Spain	9.9
Trinidad and Tobago	10.1
Kuwait	9.8
Qatar	9.8
Scotland	9.9

Children in Germany must be six years old by the end of June 30 to begin school in September or, upon special request, by December 31 of that year. Germany's predominant age cohort reflected this policy, spanning July 1995 through June 1996, but it also had some older and younger students in Grade 4. In Germany, policies about promotion and retention vary by *Länder* (federal state).

Next, in Figure 1, comes a group of countries where the practice is to admit children who have reached their sixth birthday by the beginning of September, when the school year begins. In these countries, which include Austria, Chinese Taipei, England, the Slovak Republic, and the United States, the predominant age cohort extended from September 1995 through to August 1996. In Austria, Chinese Taipei, and the Slovak Republic, children must be six years old on September 1 to begin primary school. Children in England must begin school at the start of the term following their fifth birthday. Age-of-entry policy and practice in the United States varies from state to state, but judging by the country's age distribution, it is common practice to admit children to school on the basis of their age at the beginning of September. Almost all of the Grade 4 students in Chinese Taipei and England were included in the predominant age cohort, reflecting strict adherence to the nationwide entrance policies and automatic promotion from grade to grade. This was less the case in Austria, the Slovak Republic, and the United States, which have, to varying degrees, promotion policies that depend on students' progress and can thus result in relatively large percentages of older students.

Figure 1 next shows Iran, where children must be six years old by September 20 to begin school, and the Netherlands, where children begin school at age six. Although their predominant age cohorts extended from October 1995 through September 1996, Iran and the Netherlands had many older students. We could have anticipated this pattern for Iran because, for each grade, students must pass an examination to be promoted. In the Netherlands, the decision is left to the schools. In Georgia and Indonesia, the predominant age cohort spanned November 1995 through October 1996, although there were also many older and younger students. The policy in Georgia is that students must have turned six by the end of December in order to enter school, while in Indonesia students can begin school at six years of age, but *must* enter by seven years of age. In Israel, where students should be age six by the beginning of the school year (which varies somewhat), the predominant age cohort extended from December 1995 through November 1996, and contained some older students and a few younger ones.

For the PIRLS 2006 countries, the most common age-of-entry practice was to admit children to primary school in the calendar year in which they turned six; for these 11 countries, the predominant age cohort coincided with the 1996 calendar year. The 11 countries included both the Flemish and French parts of Belgium, as well as France, Hong Kong SAR, Iceland, Italy, Morocco, Norway, Poland, Slovenia, and Spain. There were some slight deviations from the calendar-year policy in Hong Kong SAR, where students must be 5.8 years old by September, and in Italy, which also has an examination for early admission (perhaps explaining its somewhat younger students, on average).

Six countries in this group—Iceland, Italy, Norway, Poland, Slovenia, and Spain—had almost all of their Grade 4 students in the predominant age group. These countries reported automatic promotion, except in Slovenia, where retention can begin in the fourth grade, and in Spain, where students need to demonstrate basic competencies to be promoted. In Morocco, the distribution of students spanned a very wide range of birth months, and students were considerably older, on average, than in the other countries in this grouping. Although Morocco reported a policy of automatic promotion, it is a country striving to increase school enrollment at all levels, despite facing many economic challenges. With the exception of Morocco, and taking into account the pattern whereby fourth-graders in the countries where students enter school during the calendar year in which they turn six are typically one year younger when they enter school than are the Grade 4 students in the first group of countries shown in Figure 1 (i.e., students entering school in the calendar year in which they turn seven), it follows that students in this group of countries were among the youngest students assessed in PIRLS 2006. They were, on average, 9.9 years of age.

With respect to the remaining several countries in Figure 1, students in Trinidad and Tobago can start school when they are five years old, but the PIRLS data for this country showed quite a wide distribution of ages by birth month. Trinidad and Tobago also has a struggling economy, making it difficult to enforce educational policies. Students in Kuwait can start school if they are 5.5 years old by September, and those in Scotland can begin school between the ages of 4.5 and 6 depending on where their birth month falls in relation to the beginning of the school year in August. The students in Kuwait, Qatar, and Scotland, where the predominant age cohort extended from March 1996 through February 1997, were among the youngest of the PIRLS 2006 participants.

The information presented in Figure 1 makes apparent the considerable variation across countries in how they assign students to grades. This variation differentially influences the relationship between age and grade from country to country, making the task of comparing the effects of age and amount of schooling on achievement an extremely complicated one. In the majority of the PIRLS 2006 countries, substantial percentages of the fourth-grade students were not what Cliffordson (2007) referred to as "normal-aged" for their grade. According to Luyten (2006), application of the regression discontinuity approach presents no significant problems as long as the percentage of older and the percentage of younger students do not exceed five. However, that criterion was not met by many of the PIRLS 2006 countries.

Figure 2 presents, for each PIRLS 2006 country, the percentage of fourth-grade students included in the predominant age cohort, together with the percentage of older and younger students. The figure is organized in decreasing order by percentage of students in the predominant age cohort. The PIRLS 2006 countries in the upper part of the figure have all or practically all of their students included in a single

12-month period (e.g., from January to December or September to August), while those in the lower part have substantial percentages of older students and also some younger students.

As shown in Figure 2, eight PIRLS 2006 countries had almost all of their fourth-grade students in the predominant age cohort—95% or more in accordance with Luyten's aforementioned criterion. These countries included Iceland (100%), Norway, and England (99%), Poland (98%), Chinese Taipei (97%), Slovenia (96%), and Sweden (95%). In each case, the practice for age of entry was to admit an entire age cohort (i.e., students born in a single 12-month period) and to have automatic promotion from grade to grade, at least in the grades preceding fourth grade. Interestingly, England, Iceland, and Norway were three of the countries that Luyten (2006) studied during his analysis of the TIMSS 1995 data.

As is also evident in Figure 2, many of the participating countries had distributions that did not fit this pattern of adhering to a strict cutoff date. They instead had age distributions that featured a long tail of older students as well as some younger students. In more than half of the PIRLS 2006 countries, more than 10% of students in the grade tested were older than the students in the predominant age cohort. The most extreme examples in Figure 2 are Trinidad and Tobago, Indonesia, and Morocco, where, in particular, between one third and one half of the students were older than those in the predominant age cohort.

However, in these countries, the lack of economic development is hampering the implementation of educational policies. As noted in the *PIRLS 2006 International Report* (Mullis, Martin, Kennedy, & Foy, 2007), the majority of the countries had a Human Development Index (HDI) of 0.9 or higher (indicating high levels of school enrollment and a good standard of living). In comparison, the relatively low HDI values for these three countries (e.g., 0.64 for Morocco) highlight the impact of economic development on students' educational achievement and, indeed, on a country's ability to implement strict policies about age of entry to school and (more generally) to increase school enrollments.

READING ACHIEVEMENT AND STUDENT AGE

If, as seems intuitive from a perspective based solely on maturation, older students within a grade would have higher reading achievement than younger students at that grade, then we could expect that countries with older students should have, on average, higher achievement than countries with younger students. As a result of the cross-national variations in age of entry and promotion and retention practices described above, the average age of students in the PIRLS 2006 countries that tested at the fourth grade ranged from 9.7 years (Italy) to 11.0 (Latvia). If being older of itself conveys an advantage in reading literacy, then the PIRLS data should show higher average reading achievement for the countries with the older students and lower average achievement for countries with younger students. However, this pattern did not appear to always be the case.

Figure 2: PIRLS 2006 average student age and age cohorts

| Country | Percentage of students | | | Older students | Predominant age cohort and younger students |
	Older than the predominant age cohort	In the predominant age cohort	Younger than the predominant age cohort		
Iceland	0 (0.1)	100 (0.1)	0 (0.1)		
Norway	0 (0.1)	99 (0.2)	0 (0.1)		
England	1 (0.1)	99 (0.4)	1 (0.4)		
Poland	1 (0.2)	98 (0.3)	1 (0.1)		
Chinese Taipei	1 (0.2)	97 (0.3)	2 (0.2)		
Slovenia	2 (0.2)	96 (0.3)	2 (0.2)		
Sweden	3 (0.4)	95 (0.5)	2 (0.3)		
Italy	3 (0.4)	93 (0.6)	4 (0.6)		
Scotland	7 (1.0)	93 (1.0)	0 (0.1)		
Spain	8 (0.7)	91 (0.8)	1 (0.2)		
Israel	8 (0.6)	89 (0.6)	3 (0.2)		
Bulgaria	7 (0.9)	88 (1.1)	5 (0.6)		
Hong Kong (SAR)	15 (1.1)	85 (1.1)	0 (0.0)		
Belgium (Flemish)	14 (0.9)	85 (0.9)	2 (0.2)		
Kuwait	13 (0.7)	84 (0.7)	3 (0.3)		
Denmark	12 (0.6)	84 (0.7)	4 (0.4)		
Lithuania	7 (0.5)	84 (0.7)	9 (0.5)		
Slovakia	15 (0.8)	84 (0.8)	1 (0.1)		
Austria	16 (0.7)	82 (0.7)	2 (0.3)		
Iran	18 (1.2)	82 (1.2)	0 (0.1)		
France	16 (1.0)	81 (1.0)	2 (0.3)		
Macedonia	9 (0.7)	80 (0.9)	10 (0.7)		
Moldova	13 (0.8)	80 (0.9)	7 (0.7)		
Belgium (French)	18 (0.9)	80 (1.0)	2 (0.3)		
Romania	14 (0.9)	79 (1.2)	7 (1.1)		
Latvia	16 (0.8)	79 (1.2)	5 (1.0)		
Hungary	17 (1.0)	77 (1.0)	6 (0.5)		
United States	15 (1.3)	77 (1.2)	8 (0.7)		
Germany	15 (1.3)	77 (1.2)	8 (0.5)		
Georgia	18 (1.1)	76 (1.0)	6 (0.6)		
Netherlands	21 (1.5)	75 (1.4)	4 (0.4)		
Qatar	21 (0.5)	74 (0.5)	6 (0.3)		
Russian Federation	11 (0.6)	73 (1.1)	16 (1.0)		
Trinidad and Tobago	33 (1.5)	60 (1.4)	8 (0.7)		
Indonesia	42 (1.9)	50 (1.7)	8 (0.5)		
Morocco	50 (1.4)	46 (1.3)	4 (0.4)		

50% 0% 50% 100%

21

Figure 3 plots, for each PIRLS 2006 country shown in Figures 1 and 2, average reading achievement against the average age of the PIRLS 2006 students. The Pearson correlation between age and achievement for these 36 countries is 0.15, which is only slightly positive. But what is important to observe here is that the countries with developing economies tended to have older students, as evidenced by Morocco. As another example (not included in Figure 3), South Africa (with a low HDI value of 0.65) participated in PIRLS 2006 at Grade 5 and had the oldest students, on average, at 11.9 years old. Yet, despite its students being a year older than even the oldest group of fourth-grade participants and having experienced one more year of school, South Africa had the lowest average achievement across all the countries. Thus, it appears that degree of economic development can have a much larger impact on educational achievement than can age-within-grade or even amount of schooling.

AGE-WITHIN-GRADE AND STUDENT READING ACHIEVEMENT

Many factors other than average age can influence a country's average reading achievement. As such, there are many possible explanations for why a simple plot of countries' average achievement against average age might not show an expected positive relationship. For example, and as we have already noted, economic development and the investment in education that this makes possible may have a stronger effect on literacy levels than average age of students at a grade level. However, even if there is an underlying maturational effect, that is, older students being more able than younger, it is possible that the combined effect of a country's policy and practice on age of entry to primary school together with its promotion and retention policies could disrupt this expected positive relationship between age and achievement.

Figures 1 and 2 above showed many examples of countries with sizeable percentages of PIRLS 2006 fourth graders who were older than the predominant age cohort. In general, these countries have policies that result in students being retained and repeating a grade. In a country where students have to demonstrate a certain level of progress in order to be promoted to the next grade, the weaker students who have to repeat a grade will be older, on average, than the students who are in that grade for the first time. Similarly, in a country where children are not obliged to begin school strictly on the basis of age, there may be a tendency for parents to hold back for another year those children they consider not quite ready for the rigors of schooling. Some of these students also may turn out to be among the less able of their age cohort. These factors, operating separately or in combination, can create a situation in which the older students in a grade level are also among the academically less able. If sufficiently large numbers of such students are involved, this factor can affect the relationship between age and achievement within the grade.

The first part of this study has shown that the distribution of students' ages within fourth grade varied very widely across the PIRLS 2006 countries, with many societal and systemic factors coming into play. Despite this variation, we identified a number of countries where the policy appeared to be to admit children to school solely on the

Figure 3: PIRLS 2006 Grade 4 average reading achievement by average age

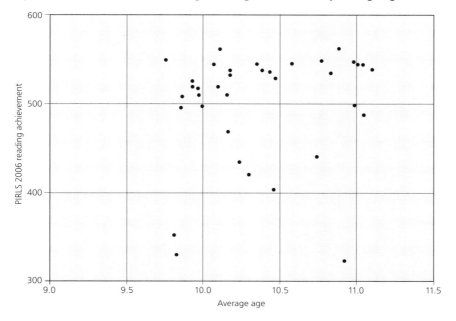

basis of their chronological age, and to automatically promote this cohort through the grades, at least as far as Grade 4. Based on the findings of previous research, we could assume that any underlying "natural" or maturational relationship between age and achievement would be most apparent in such countries—those where all the students in the grade come from a single one-year age cohort and where there has been no grade repetition for weaker students or promotion for high-performing students. We selected, from the eight PIRLS 2006 countries with age distributions meeting these criteria (see Figure 4), Iceland, Norway, and England, in order to explore this issue. These three countries had the greatest percentages of target-grade students (essentially all students) in the predominant age cohort, and all three have the policy of promoting primary-school students automatically from one grade to the next.

For Iceland, Norway, and England, Figure 4 presents the percentage of students at each birth-month of the predominant age cohort, together with average reading achievement for each month. When reading across this figure for each country, we can see that the younger students are to the left and the older students to the right. The bars representing the percentages of students at each month of birth are labeled accordingly (e.g., "9612" refers to the year 1996 and the month of December, or December 1996). Students younger than those in the predominant age cohort are represented by the bar labeled "Yng" and those older by the bar labeled "Old."

As is evident in Figure 4, each of the three countries has an approximately uniform distribution of students across the 12 months of the predominant age cohort and very few younger or older students. Accompanying the percentage of students

Figure 4: Example countries with all or almost all students in the predominant age cohort: Iceland, Norway, England

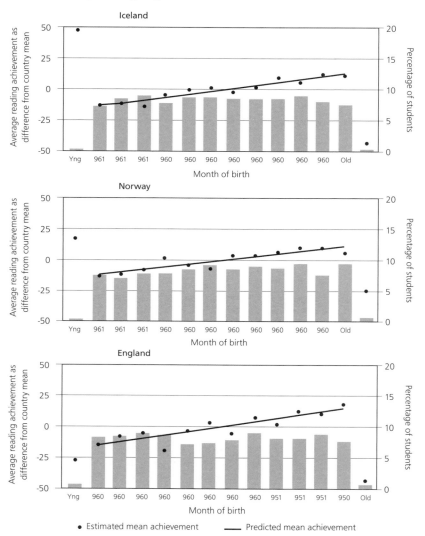

at each birth month is the average reading achievement for the students at each birth month, expressed as a difference from the overall mean for the country. The left side of the display for each country presents a scale ranging from -50 to +50, with 0 indicating the country's overall mean reading achievement. The black dot for each month shows the degree to which students with that birth-month had average achievement below or above the overall mean for the country. For all three countries, the achievement pattern is the same: average reading achievement is lowest among the younger students and gradually increases as students get older. Therefore, as shown by the regression line, there is a positive relationship between age and reading achievement. The very small percentages of students who were younger or older than the predominant age cohort have little impact on the age–achievement relationship, even though the very youngest students have the highest achievement and the very oldest have the lowest achievement.

The display for Germany, the United States, and Austria in Figure 5 provides a contrasting example. These countries are three of the many PIRLS 2006 countries that had a relatively large percentage of students older than the predominant age cohort. In Austria, Germany, and the United States, approximately 15% of the Grade 4 students assessed were older than the predominant age cohort (see Figure 2). Additionally, in Germany and the United States, eight percent of the students were younger than the predominant cohort, and in Austria, two percent. In all three countries, the older students had average achievement well below the students in the predominant age cohort, and the younger students had achievement above them, at least in Austria and Germany. Furthermore, the achievement pattern evident in Figure 4, that is, higher achievement among the older students in the predominant age cohort, is not evident in Figure 5. It appears that, in countries such as these, the combined effect of entry and promotion and retention practices is that of producing a predominant age cohort with uniform reading achievement, together with an older group with lower achievement and a (smaller) younger group with higher achievement. Note that the regression lines in Figure 5 are based on students in the predominant age cohort only. Including the younger and older students would have made the age–achievement relationships even less positive, and somewhat distorted.

Consideration of the information presented in Figures 4 and 5 makes clear that no simple, consistent relationship within a grade level between student age and reading achievement applied to all countries at fourth grade. This finding implies that any attempt to make a global statistical adjustment to countries' average achievement in order to account for differences in average age is likely to be misleading.

GROWTH IN READING ACHIEVEMENT FROM FOURTH TO FIFTH GRADE

In this last section of this paper, we provide an example of how the regression discontinuity approach can be applied to the PIRLS 2006 data. As shown in Figure 4, Iceland and Norway were two of the countries with strict adherence to an age-of-entry cutoff and automatic promotion through the grades. In addition, Iceland and Norway were the two countries that administered the PIRLS 2006 assessment at the fifth grade as well as at the fourth grade. Although the fifth-grade samples were somewhat smaller than the fourth-grade samples reported internationally for PIRLS 2006, the fifth-grade samples were nationally representative and so provided us with an opportunity to examine the relationship between age, grade, and reading achievement (for information on the fifth-grade samples, see Martin, Mullis, & Kennedy, 2007).

Figure 5: Example countries with students older or younger that in the predominant age cohort: Germany, United States, Austria

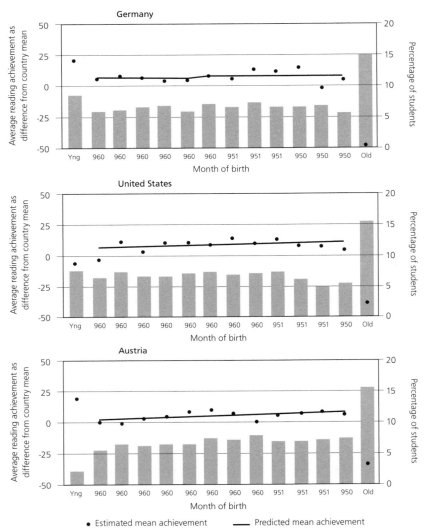

Figures 6, 7, and 8 summarize the results of the series of regression analyses that we conducted in order to model the relationship between age-within-grade (represented by birth-month) and reading achievement for Iceland and Norway. Model 1 in Figure 6 shows the regression coefficients resulting from fitting separate equations to the fourth- and fifth-grade data in each country. The slopes of the regression lines in this model for the fourth and fifth grades are approximately parallel (2.5 and 2.2, respectively, for Iceland, and 2.1 and 2.9, respectively, for Norway). Accordingly, for this exploratory analysis, we decided to fit parallel slopes for the next step, as shown in Figure 6, Model 2. The parallel slopes for the two regression lines imply that the relationship between age and reading achievement is the same in the fourth and fifth grades in each country.

The fitted lines with parallel slopes are presented graphically in Figure 6, which also shows average reading achievement by birth month for fourth and fifth grade for both Iceland and Norway. Fitting separate lines with parallel slopes to fourth and fifth grade (2.3 for Iceland and 2.5 for Norway) provides estimates of the average difference in reading achievement between the two grades. These are 38.3 score points for Iceland and 42.3 points for Norway (see Figure 6, Model 2). According to the parallel-slopes model, the fifth-grade students in Iceland scored 38.3 points higher, on average, than the fourth-grade students on the PIRLS 2006 assessment, while the fifth-graders in Norway scored 42.3 points higher than the fourth-graders. These estimates are reasonably close to the actual differences between the grades: 40 points for Iceland and 37.4 points for Norway (Figure 6, Model 1).

The approximately 40-points difference in the reading achievement of the fourth- and fifth-grade students is an estimate of the average growth in achievement that could be expected in these two countries as students move from the fourth through to the fifth grade. This increase is less than that found by Luyten (2006) with respect to the TIMSS mathematics and science data. However, we could anticipate that the increase in reading achievement would be less because students have essentially learned the basics of reading by fourth grade but would still be developing their mathematics skills between third and fourth grades.

Figure 6: PIRLS 2006 reading achievement as a function of birth month within grade

Model 1: Reading achievement by birth-month, separate models by grade

Country	Grade	Intercept		Slope	
Iceland	4	496.8	(2.09)	2.5	(0.33)
	5	536.8	(5.21)	2.2	(0.59)
Norway	4	486.2	(3.59)	2.1	(0.43)
	5	523.6	(7.48)	2.9	(1.32)

Model 2: Reading achievement by birth month, parallel regression lines

Country	Intercept		Grade		Slope	
Iceland	497.6	(2.06)	38.3	(3.69)	2.3	(0.33)
Norway	483.7	(4.69)	42.3	(4.23)	2.5	(0.71)

Model 3: Reading achievement by birth month, extended regression lines

Country	Intercept		Grade		Slope	
Iceland	497.6	(2.06)	10.3	(5.81)	2.3	(0.33)
Norway	483.7	(4.69)	12.1	(9.10)	2.5	(0.71)

This growth in reading achievement reflects not only the effects of an extra year of schooling but also other learning experiences in the home and the community as well as cognitive maturation as the students became a year older. These factors are inextricably interwoven, because all the students attended school for a year and, at the same time, all the students grew older and more mature. Therefore, it is not possible from data such as these to say with any certainty how much of the 40-points growth from fourth grade to fifth grade in Iceland and Norway can be attributed to the effects of a year of schooling and how much can be attributed to other, incidental maturational factors. However, the regression discontinuity technique makes it possible to capitalize on the common relationship between age and reading achievement in these two grades to estimate the effect of schooling in these countries.

The predominant age cohort for the PIRLS 2006 fourth-grade students in Iceland and Norway was the cohort born between January 1 and December 31, 1996; the corresponding cohort for the fifth-grade students was those students born between January 1 and December 31, 1995. As Figure 7 shows, there was a steady increase in average reading achievement at fourth grade from the youngest students (those born in December 1996) to the oldest students (those born in January 1996) and also at fifth grade from the youngest students (those born in December 1995) to the oldest students (those born in January 1995). Because the regression lines for the two grades in the figure are parallel within each country, the increases from month to month at fourth grade are the same and the increases from month to month at fifth grade are the same.

Figure 7 depicts average achievement for the two grade levels along a continuous two-year birth-month continuum, beginning on the left with those born in December 1996 (the youngest fourth-grade students), and extending on the right to those born in January 1995 (the oldest fifth-grade students). The cutoff point for the two grades is between January 1996 and December 1995. A discontinuity in the regression lines at this point would indicate an achievement difference associated with a change from fourth to fifth grade, whereas a continuous straight line would imply no discernable grade effect.

For both Iceland and Norway, Figure 8 shows a discontinuity in the fitted regression line, with higher achievement associated with fifth grade in both countries. For Iceland, the grade effect, adjusted for birth month, was 10.3 score points; for Norway, it was 12.1 points (see Figure 6, Model 3). One interpretation of this finding with respect to Iceland is that we could expect the extra year of schooling to give a hypothetical fifth-grade student born in a particular birth month a 10.3-point advantage over a hypothetical fourth-grade student born in the same birth month. Similarly, in Norway, we could expect that a hypothetical fifth-grade student would have a 12.1-point advantage over a hypothetical fourth-grade student born in the same month.

Essentially, the foregoing analysis implies that the 38.3-point difference between the average reading achievement of the fourth- and fifth-grade students in Iceland could be separated into a 10.3-point grade effect and a 28-point age-within-grade effect,

Figure 7: PIRLS 2006 reading achievement as a function of birth month at Grades 4 and 5: Iceland and Norway

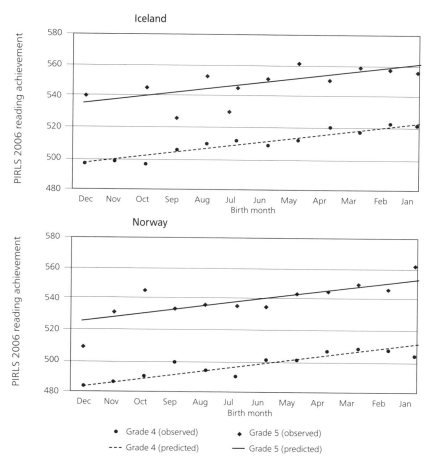

while the 42.3-point difference in Norway could be separated into a 12.1-points grade effect and a 30.2-point age-within-grade effect.

When considering this finding, it is important to recognize that the relative sizes of the grade effect and the age-within-grade effect are determined by the slopes of the age-within-grade regression lines. The steeper the slopes of the regression lines for each grade, the more the lines will align across the grades and the smaller will be the estimate of the grade effect. However, as we demonstrated earlier, the slopes of the age-within-grade regression lines are greatly influenced by the factors that determine the distribution of age-within-grade. And, as we also observed earlier, Iceland and Norway are two of the countries where age alone is the criterion for beginning school. In both countries, the relationship between age and achievement within grade was positive.

Figure 8: PIRLS 2006 reading achievement as a function of birth month across Grades 4 and 5 consecutively: Iceland and Norway

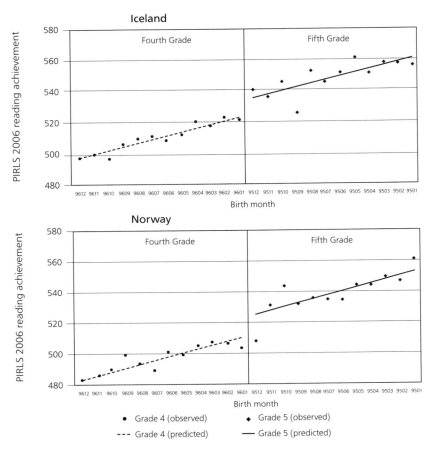

DISCUSSION AND CONCLUSION

Analyses by Cliffordson (2008), Cliffordson and Gustafsson (2010), and Luyten and Valdecamp (2008) have demonstrated the promise of new, powerful analytic techniques for disentangling the effects of age and grade in large-scale cross-sectional student achievement data. However, these methods can depend on restrictive assumptions about the relationship between age and grade, as is the case for the regression discontinuity technique used in several important studies (Cahan & Cohen, 1987; Cliffordson & Gustafsson 2007; Luyten, 2006). Even when recent investigations that relax these assumptions, such as the Heckman approach applied by Luyten and Valdecamp, or the instrumental variables regression approach of Cliffordson and Gustafsson, are taken into account, these approaches require use of adjacent grade data from countries where it is possible to explicitly model the relationship between age and grade. The present study has shown that although the relationship between age and grade may be straightforward and amenable to analysis in some countries, in general the complexity of the age–grade relationship remains a barrier to the application of any straightforward adjustment for the effects of age differences to the grade-level achievement results reported by TIMSS and PIRLS.

We used PIRLS 2006 reading achievement data for fourth-grade students to conduct the age-by-birth-month analysis for 36 countries. The analysis showed that variation in policies of age of entry to school resulted in different average ages for the fourth-grade students from country to country. In line with the three most prevalent policies across the participating PIRLS countries, the oldest fourth-grade students in the assessment were from countries that admit students in the calendar year in which they turn seven, the next oldest from countries that admit children who have reached their sixth birthday by September, and the youngest from countries where students begin primary school in the calendar year in which they turn six. Promotion and retention policies also vary across the PIRLS countries to the extent that some of the PIRLS 2006 countries had a relatively large percentage of "older" students by fourth grade. Thus, students who were retained and repeated grades were older than the predominant age cohort for their grade. Finally, students in several of the countries facing challenges associated with economic development were older, on average, than the average age of their international peers.

With so many factors influencing the within-grade age distribution, the finding that the relationship at fourth grade between students' age and their reading achievement differed across the PIRLS 2006 countries is understandable. In the relatively few countries with strict age cutoffs for entering school and policies of automatic promotion, students were equally distributed by birth month across the fourth grade. In these countries, the older fourth-graders had systematically higher average reading achievement than the younger students. However, in the many countries with relatively large percentages of older students, these students had lower reading achievement than the younger students. Thus, across the PIRLS 2006 countries at fourth grade, there was only a slightly positive correlation (0.15) between age and reading achievement. Also, the PIRLS 2006 countries with the fewest economic resources tended to have the oldest students and the lowest average reading achievement, a finding that highlights the dominant importance of economic development for students' educational achievement.

TIMSS' and PIRLS' choice of grade as the basis for monitoring and reporting student achievement makes student age an important contextual variable to consider when interpreting achievement differences across countries. This choice also means, however, that participating countries can monitor the relationship between changes in policies related to students' ages within grades and improvements (or declines) in average achievement. For example, both the Russian Federation and Slovenia have lowered the age of entry into school to provide an extra year of primary school (now four years of schooling rather than three) for their students. In both cases, the increase in schooling has coincided with an increase in average reading achievement (Mullis, Martin, Kennedy, & Foy, 2007).

Because Iceland and Norway are two countries that admit children to school strictly on the basis of age and automatically promote them through the grades, these two countries, by assessing two grades in PIRLS 2006 (fifth as well as fourth grade), were able to examine the relationship between age-within-grade and reading achievement using the regression discontinuity approach. They were also able to examine these results in the light of existing curricular emphases and prevalent instructional approaches to reading.

This study has shown that the interrelationships among achievement, grade, and age vary from country to country and often are extremely complicated. These complications are rooted in countries' policies on age of school entry, on promotion and retention, and on how each country actually implements—in accordance with its economic, social, and cultural contexts—these policies in practice. Some countries adopt a strict policy of admitting students to primary school solely on the basis of age and maintain the resulting age distribution by way of automatic promotion through the grades. Others allow parents some latitude in choosing when to have their child begin school, and may permit or require students who are struggling to repeat a year. The study also has shown that the policies that countries implement with regard to these issues are reflected in the distributions of students' ages within grade and in the relationship between age and reading achievement at fourth grade.

References

Cahan, S., & Cohen, N. (1989). Age versus schooling effects on intelligence development. *Child Development*, *60*(5), 1239–1249.

Cliffordson, C. (2008, September). *Effects of schooling and age on performance in mathematics and science: A between-grade regression discontinuity design applied to Swedish TIMSS 1995 data*. Paper presented at the third IEA International Research Conference (IRC-2008), Taipei, Taiwan.

Cliffordson, C., & Gustafsson, J.-E. (2007). Effects of age and schooling on intellectual performance: Estimates obtained from analysis of continuous variation in age and length of schooling. *Intelligence*, *36*(2), 143–152.

Cliffordson, C., & Gustafsson, J.-E. (2010). *Effects of schooling and age on performance in mathematics and science: A between-grade regression discontinuity design with instrumental variables applied to Swedish TIMSS 1995 data*. Paper presented at the fourth IEA International Research Conference (IRC-2010), Gothenburg, Sweden.

Foy, P., & Kennedy, A. M. (Eds.). (2008). *PIRLS 2006 user guide*. Chestnut Hill, MA: TIMSS & PIRLS International Study Center, Boston College.

Heckman, J. J. (1979). Sample selection bias as a specification error. *Econometrica, 51*, 153–161.

Kennedy, A. M., Mullis, I. V. S., Martin, M. O., & Trong, K. L. (Eds.). (2007). *PIRLS 2006 encyclopedia*. Chestnut Hill, MA: TIMSS & PIRLS International Study Center, Boston College.

Luyten, H. (2006). An empirical assessment of the absolute effect of schooling: Regression-discontinuity applied to TIMSS 1995. *Oxford Review of Education*, *32*, 397–429.

Luyten, H., Peschar, J., & Coe, R. (2008). Effects of schooling on reading performance, reading engagement, and reading activities of 15-year-olds in England. *American Educational Research Journal*, *45*(2), 319–342.

Luyten, H., & Veldkamp, B. (2008, September). *Assessing the effect of schooling with cross-sectional data: Between grade differences addressed as a selection-bias problem*. Paper presented at the third IEA International Research Conference (IRC-2008), Taipei, Taiwan.

Martin, M. O., Mullis, I. V. S., & Kennedy, A. M. (Eds.). (2007). *PIRLS 2006 technical report*. Chestnut Hill, MA: TIMSS & PIRLS International Study Center, Boston College.

Mullis, I. V. S., Martin, M. O., & Foy, P., with Olson, J. F., Preuschoff, A. C., Erberber, E., ... Galia, J. (2008). *TIMSS 2007 international mathematics report: Findings from IEA's Trends in International Mathematics and Science Study at the fourth and eighth grades*. Chestnut Hill, MA: TIMSS & PIRLS International Study Center, Boston College.

Mullis, I. V. S., Martin, M. O., Kennedy, A. M., & Foy, P. (2007). *PIRLS 2006 international report: IEA's Progress in International Reading Literacy Study in primary schools in 40 countries*. Chestnut Hill, MA: TIMSS & PIRLS International Study Center, Boston College.

Mullis, I. V. S., Martin, M. O., Olson, J. F., Berger, D. R., Milne, D., & Stanco, G. M. (Eds.). (2008). *TIMSS 2007 encyclopedia: A guide to mathematics and science education around the world*. Chestnut Hill, MA: TIMSS & PIRLS International Study Center, Boston College.

Organisation for Economic Co-operation and Development (OECD). (2001). *Knowledge and skills for life: First results from the OECD Programme for International Student Assessment (PISA) 2000*. Paris, France: Author.

Van Damme, J., Vanhee, L., & Pustjens, H. (2008, September). *Explaining reading achievement in PIRLS by age and SES*. Paper presented at the third IEA International Research Conference (IRC-2008), Taipei, Taiwan.

The influences of home language, gender, and social class on mathematics literacy in France, Germany, Hong Kong, and the United States

Aminah Perkins, Laura Quaynor, and George Engelhard, Jr.
Division of Educational Studies, Emory University, Atlanta, Georgia, USA

The purpose of this study was to examine the influences of home language, gender, and social class on mathematical literacy within the context of four countries (France, Germany, Hong Kong, and the United States) whose students participated in the mathematics section of the 2003 Programme for International Student Assessment (PISA). Rasch (1980) measurement theory was used to examine the effects of the three independent variables on students' performance on the mathematics test items; particular attention was paid to home language. Use of differential group (DGF) and differential person functioning (DPF) provided additional detail regarding variation and aberrant responses on the test of 84 items related to mathematical literacy. Home language had a statistically significant effect in Germany and Hong Kong, but not in France and the United States. As expected, gender and social class had statistically significant effects in all four countries on mathematics literacy, with the exception of gender in France. The DGF and DPF analyses illustrated group and individual variations in item responses related to home language within France.

IERI Monograph Series: Issues and Methodologies in Large-Scale Assessments Volume 4
Copyright © 2011 by Educational Testing Service and International Association for the Evaluation of Educational Achievement.

INTRODUCTION

Large-scale international assessments provide rich data that allow researchers to explore the relationships among different variables within a variety of national contexts. Different countries serve as a social laboratory where scholars can explore the connections between variables such as gender, race, social class, and school achievement. In this study, we used data from the mathematics section of the Organisation for Economic Co-operation and Development (OECD)'s Programme for International Student Assessment (PISA) 2003 for four of the participating countries—France, Germany, Hong Kong, and the United States—in order to investigate relationships among home language, gender, social class, and mathematical literacy.

We were also interested in identifying individuals and groups of students within these four countries whose response patterns on PISA 2003 were dissimilar to those of other students with comparable levels of mathematical literacy. We therefore designed our study so that we could explore differential person functioning (DPF).[1] We particularly wanted to know if some students' mathematics literacy might not have been accurately assessed because their home language differed from the test language, and if patterns of performance on the mathematics items were differentiated according to student gender and social class. Furthermore, we sought to identify students whose person response functions (PRFs) were dissimilar to the PRFs of other students with similar achievement levels. In some instances, a student can be so unlike other examinees that his or her overall test score is not an appropriate representation of his or her mathematical literacy (Levine & Rubin, 1979).

When conducting our secondary analyses of the PISA 2003 data for the four countries, we investigated the following four research questions; the fourth provided the main focus of our study.

1. Is there a relationship between mathematics achievement and assessment of students in their home language?

2. Is there a relationship between mathematics achievement and gender?

3. Is there a relationship between mathematics achievement and social class?

4. Can we use person response functions to examine data-to-model fit for individuals and groups?

We also explored the interactions between home language, gender, and social class.

---

1   We explain this term and the related term "person response functions" on page 39–40.

RELEVANT LITERATURE

Mathematics Achievement and Home Language

Mathematics is the school subject that teachers and researchers tend to view as the subject most accessible to linguistic minority students (see, for example, Rolka, 2004). As such, we hypothesized that mathematics was the subject least likely to differentiate the performance of linguistic minority and linguistic majority students. Although not all linguistic minority students are immigrants and not all immigrant students belong to linguistic minorities, it is often the case that students who are immigrants are also in the linguistic minority. In this section, we discuss results from PISA testing that are relevant to both groups of students.

PISA reports unique patterns of achievement and immigrant status within different countries. For example, in France and Germany, students with an immigrant background are more likely than students without an immigrant background to perform at the lower levels of achievement, while in Australia and Macau (China), the two groups have similar levels of mathematical literacy (OECD, 2006). However, of more importance than the differences in academic performance between nonimmigrant and immigrant students is the limited academic performance of many of the latter group of students. In some countries, large proportions of both first- and second-generation immigrant students[2] do not achieve a basic level of mathematics proficiency. For example, only 40% of first-generation immigrant students in France and 25% of such students in Germany reached Level 2 on the PISA achievement scale—"a baseline level of mathematics proficiency ... at which students begin to demonstrate the kind of skills that enable them to actively use mathematics; for example they are able to use basic algorithms, formulae and procedures, to make literal interpretations and to apply direct reasoning" (OECD, 2006, p. 8). In Germany and the United States, only one-third of second-generation immigrant students reached Level 2, raising questions about the ability of schools not only to adequately prepare all students as mathematically literate adults but also to assimilate these children socially. Another possible explanation is that immigrants within the different countries vary in the extent of their previous academic attainment.

The OECD (2006) reports that student home language accounted for some of the differences in mathematics achievement on the PISA 2003 test between immigrant and non-immigrant students in some countries. After controlling for parents' educational and occupational status, the PISA researchers found that the performance gap associated with the language spoken at home remained significant in Belgium, Canada, Germany, Hong Kong, Macau, the Russian Federation, and the United States. Within this group, achievement differences between students who spoke the language of the test at home and students who did not ranged from 13 achievement scale score points in Canada through 46 points in the United States to 90 points in Germany (Miller, Sen, & Malley, 2007).

---

2 First-generation immigrant students are students who were born abroad. Second-generation students are students born in the country of residence but with one or both parents born abroad.

Mathematics Achievement and Gender

Many countries continue to report differences in mathematics achievement between male and female students, with the differences generally favoring males. This gap, however, has diminished in recent years (Liu & Wilson, 2009a; Mullis, Martin, Gonzalez, & Chrostowski, 2004; OECD, 2004). Of the 41 countries that participated in PISA 2003, 12 showed no significant gender differences in mathematics literacy, 27 revealed a gender difference in favor of males, and one (Iceland) reported a gender difference in favor of females (OECD, 2004). In some contexts within and across countries, no gender differences emerged between boys' and girls' responses to certain types of mathematics items, although gender differences remained with respect to items in other formats or focused on specific mathematical domains (OECD, 2004; Robertson, 2005).

Liu and Wilson (2009b) drew on PISA 2003 data to compare the mathematics performance of students in the United States and Hong Kong. They found no gender differences in the United States for multiple-choice items. In Hong Kong, however, males outperformed female students on the same items. In the United States, female students outperformed male students on items related to probability, but in Hong Kong, there was no statistically significant difference between male and female students on these same items. These performance differences related to gender were, however, small compared to the differences in mathematics achievement overall between students in the United States and students in Hong Kong.

Else-Quest, Hyde, and Linn (2010) showed that mathematics achievement on PISA and on the International Association for the Evaluation of Educational Achievement's (IEA's) Trends in International Mathematics and Science Study (TIMSS) was related to other contextual indicators of societal gender differences. Lower female mathematics achievement was associated with lower female representation in government, research, and economic activity. Similarly, van Langen, Bosker, and Dekkers (2006) reported that female participation in science, technology, engineering, and mathematics (STEM) careers was higher in countries where the performance of female students was relatively close to that of male students on PISA. The authors of the PISA 2003 report (OECD, 2004) suggested that student attitudes toward mathematics may also have been associated with performance on the PISA 2003 test.

Mathematics Achievement and Social Class

Although social class is a difficult variable to define across national contexts, PISA collects information about the occupations of students' parents that can help to serve as a proxy for social class. The International Labor Office (ILO) provides an international framework for occupations, which PISA researchers use to code the parental occupational status of students.[3] These occupational codes are then cross-referenced to the International Socio-Economic Index (ISEI) (Ganzeboom & Treiman, 1996).

---

3 If both parents are in paid employment, PISA uses the higher occupational status of the two as the index of social status.

Student performance in mathematics on PISA 2003 strongly related to parental occupational status. Each standard deviation of difference on the ISEI was associated with 34 points of difference on the PISA mathematics scale (OECD, 2004). Some countries reported larger differences in student achievement based on parental occupation than did others. In Belgium, France, Germany, Hungary, Luxembourg, the Slovak Republic, and Liechtenstein, students whose parents had the lowest-status jobs scored similarly to students in the lowest-performing countries (OECD, 2004). This relationship was mediated by between-school performance differences. Overall, students at schools serving a majority of students from lower socioeconomic status (SES) homes performed at much lower levels in mathematics than low-SES students attending schools where the majority of students came from high SES backgrounds (Carey, 2008; Marks, 2006; OECD, 2004).

Precision of Person Measurement

We used differential person functioning (DPF) to identify students and groups of students whose performance on the PISA 2003 mathematics items differed from the performance expected under the Rasch (1980) model of analysis. DPF occurs when an individual's observed response pattern differs from the expected response pattern for individuals with the same measured latent trait. When an individual's response pattern is unlike what would be expected given the model of analysis, we refer to his or her responses as "unexpected."

The notion of person invariance is not new and dates back to the work of early researchers such as Mosier (1940, 1941). Person fit, or the variability in person responses on a particular test, is of considerable importance: if individual students' response patterns are unexpected, then using their total score on a test to represent their mathematical literacy is likely to be misleading. This concern with respect to person reliability is a theme evident across the works of Keats (1967), Lumsden (1977, 1980), and Mosier (1940, 1941).

The functional relationship between the probability of a person giving a correct response and his or her actual achievement level can be graphically represented through the use of a person response function (PRF). Graphical depictions of this relationship can be traced back to the work of Weiss (1973) and Lumsden (1977). Weiss called his graphical representation of item difficulties and individual responses to items a "trace line": his proposal was that as items increase in difficulty, the percentage of responses that a person is likely to answer correctly decreases. Lumsden (1977, 1980), who used psychological measurement and mental growth as the backdrop for his work, provided a useful approach to addressing issues of person reliability. He introduced the use of the person characteristic curve (PCC), equivalent to what is referred to as a PRF in this study: "The person characteristic curve is the plot for a single subject of the proportion of items passed at different difficulty levels. It is perfectly analogous to the item characteristic curve" (Lumsden, 1977, p. 478).

Lumsden was the first researcher to clearly define this term, although the idea was implicit in previous research by Keats (1967), Vale and Weiss (1975), and Weiss (1973).

The underlying idea behind PRFs is that a person receives a correct response on an item when his or her location on a latent variable is greater than the given location of an item. PRFs are concerned with an individual's response to items representing various difficulty levels, in contrast to item response functions (IRFs), where the focus is on the response of individuals who, as a group, will exhibit different levels of achievement on one specific item (Carroll, 1983; Mosier, 1940, 1941).

Lumsden (1977, 1980) also identified issues associated with using a total test score for grouping individuals. For example, two students may receive the same total test score, but when their scores are examined in relation to their correct responses on items that are ordered by difficulty, their person response functions will cross. This crossing illustrates the impact of the individuals' different response patterns. As Lumsden (1977, p. 481) states, the crossing of PRFs results in the estimates of reliability being "biased by the difficulty of the items." For teachers, knowing which situations can lead to crossing of PRFs could help them determine the instructional strategies most suitable for individual students.

Performances exhibiting crossing PRFs can lead to problems with the substantive interpretation of person performance. The ordering of persons below and above the intersection points vary when PRFs cross (Perkins & Engelhard, 2009). If PRFs do not cross, then persons are ordered in the same way across item subsets, thereby achieving item-invariant measurement. Crossing PRFs, however, yield person ordering that varies as a function of the difficulty of the item subsets. Our study provides illustrations regarding the potential utility and substantive value of PRFs.

METHOD

The PISA Assessment

PISA, an international assessment jointly developed by the participating OECD countries, covers the domains of mathematics, reading, and science literacy. One third of the assessment items are in multiple-choice format, one third in closed constructed-response format, and one third in open constructed-response format. Results from PISA are reported as scale scores, with the scale having an average score of 500 and a standard deviation of 100. PISA uses a balanced incomplete block (BIB) design, which means that each student responds to a subset of the items, questions are shared across the subsets, and the Rasch model is used "to scale the student data to derive the various comparative measures that are produced and reported by the OECD" (Turner & Adams, 2007, p. 246).

The mathematics section of PISA was designed to evaluate mathematical literacy, defined by the OECD (2003, p. 15) as "an individual's capacity to identify and understand the role that mathematics plays in the world, to make well-founded judgments and to use and engage with mathematics in ways that meet the needs of that individual's life as a constructive, concerned and reflective citizen." PISA 2003 contained 84 mathematics items divided into four content domains (space and shape, quantity, uncertainty, and change and relationship) and described mathematics literacy on a scale comprising three competency clusters.

Because Rasch measurement models enable the development of measurement scales in the form of a line or a variable map, test items, such as those in PISA, can be placed along this line according to their levels of difficulty. Individuals can also be placed on this line according to their level of achievement. In Rasch measurement, this construction is referred to as a variable map. Figure 1 displays the scale for mathematics literacy as a variable map identifying the expected and hypothesized location of students and mathematics items.

Students participating in PISA also fill out a questionnaire that asks them to report personal and family characteristics. Students self-identify the language spoken at home, as well as such characteristics as parental occupation, educational level, and attitudes toward school (OECD, 2003). This information enabled us to determine whether or not the item difficulty locations were invariant across the language, gender, and social groups within the four countries that we considered.

Figure 1: Hypothesized variable map

Latent variable: mathematical literacy

Logit scale	Students	Item
HIGH 5.00 4.00 3.00	• Interpret more complex information and negotiate a number of processing steps	*Reflection* • Original mathematical approach • Multiple complex methods • Generalization
2.00 1.00 0.00 -1.00	• Typically carry out more complex tasks involving more than a single processing step	*Connections* • Standard problem-solving, translation, and interpretation
-2.00 -3.00 -4.00 -5.00 LOW	• Typically carry out single-step processes that involve recognition of familiar contexts and mathematically well-formulated problems and reproduction of well-known mathematical facts or processes	*Reproduction* • Routine computations, procedures, and problem-solving

Participants

PISA 2003 was administered to students between 15.3 and 16.2 years of age. Representative samples of at least 4,500 students were selected from at least 150 schools within each of the 41 countries that participated in the mathematics assessment. Table 1 displays the demographic characteristics of the students from the four countries featured in our study. The number of students across the four countries was 18,894, with 4,300 in France, 4,660 in Germany, 4,778 in Hong Kong, and 5,456 in the United States. As is recommended for researchers conducting comparative analyses of data sets from various countries, we used senate weights to adjust the calibration weight of each country to the same sample size (M. von Davier, personal communication, December 25, 2010). In line with Rutkowski, Gonzalez, Joncas, and von Davier's (2010) recommendation for analyses of large-scale survey data, we used a weight of 1,000 students per country for all of the analyses presented here.

Students speaking languages at home other than the language in which the test was administered ranged from 6.5% in France to 8.6% in the United States. According to the data on parental occupation—the variable used as a measure of SES—Hong Kong had the smallest percentage of students from white-collar highly skilled families (27.0%); the United States had the largest. The highest percentage of students from blue-collar low-skilled families was found in Hong Kong (21.5%); the lowest in the United States (4.0%). It is important to emphasize that these students self-identified their parents' occupations, which were then cross-referenced in accordance with PISA practice to the aforementioned ISEI (Ganzeboom & Treiman, 1996). Although students self-identified their parents' occupations, the trends of parental occupations across countries seemed to pair with other data related to occupational status. For example, in Hong Kong in 2003, 20% of adults were working as managerial and professional staff (Legislative Council, 2007), while in the United States, sociologists estimate that roughly half of the population comprises white-collar workers (Beeghley, 2004; Thompson & Hickey, 2005).

Country Selection

We intentionally chose France, Germany, Hong Kong, and the United States as the focus of our analyses. We wanted to consider countries with very different immigration histories and overall levels of achievement on PISA. France, as a former colonial power, receives immigrants from former colonies and follows an educational strategy of assimilation (Castles, 2004). Germany is a European state that recruited immigrants for labor after World War II, and originally provided separate schools for the children of immigrants (Castles & Miller, 2003). Although often considered an emigration society (OECD, 2006), Hong Kong has received many immigrants from mainland China (Carroll, 2007) and lost emigrants to Australia, Canada, the United Kingdom, and the United States (Salaff & Siu-Lun, 1995). In contrast, the United States is a country that was formed on the basis of immigration (OECD, 2006). Overall, students from Hong Kong scored in the top third of countries on the PISA mathematics assessment, students from Germany and France scored in the middle third, and students from the United States scored in the bottom third (OECD, 2006).

Table 1: Student characteristics

	Country							
	France (*n* = 1,000)		*Germany* (*n* = 1,000)		*Hong Kong* (*n* = 1,000)		*United States* (*n* = 1,000)	
	N	%	*N*	%	*N*	%	*N*	%
Home language								
Test language	897	89.7	803	80.3	879	87.9	873	87.3
Other language/dialect	65	6.5	67	6.7	86	8.6	86	8.6
Missing	39	3.9	130	13.0	35	3.5	41	4.1
Gender								
Male	474	47.4	498	49.8	502	50.2	504	50.4
Female	526	52.6	491	49.1	498	49.8	496	49.6
Missing	0	0.0	10	1.0	0	0.0	0	0.0
Social class								
White-collar, high-skilled	717	51.7	469	46.9	270	27.0	641	64.1
White-collar, low-skilled	229	22.9	256	25.6	328	32.8	207	20.7
Blue-collar, high-skilled	111	11.1	112	11.2	158	15.8	52	5.2
Blue-collar, low-skilled	109	10.9	71	7.1	215	21.5	40	4.0
Missing	34	3.4	92	9.2	29	2.9	59	5.9
Mathematical literacy (overall)								
M	510.9	502.99	550.38	482.89				
SE	2.50	3.32	4.54	2.95				

Note: OECD average is 500.72 (*SE* = .63). Demographic information is based on weighted data using senate weights to obtain a fixed sample size of 1,000 in each country.

Theoretical Framework

Our study was essentially an exploration of item-invariant measurement of persons and groups. Engelhard (in press) describes five requirements of invariant measurement that must be met to yield useful inferences for measurement in the social, behavioral, and health sciences:

1. The measurement of persons must be independent of the particular items that happen to be used for the measuring: *item-invariant measurement of persons*.

2. A more able person must always have a better chance of success on any item than a less able person: *non-crossing person response functions*.

3. The calibration of the items must be independent of the particular persons used for calibration: *person-invariant calibration of test items*.

4. Any person must have a better chance of success on an easy item than on a more difficult item: *non-crossing item response functions*.

5. Items must measure a single underlying latent variable: *unidimensionality*.

Requirements 1 and 2 address issues related to PRFs. These two requirements define the major focus of this study.

Data Analysis

Rasch measurement theory informed the analyses of the data. We used the FACETS computer program (Linacre, 2010) to conduct this work.[4] Figure 2 illustrates the conceptual framework underpinning our analyses. Here we can see that the latent variable of interest is mathematical literacy, made observable through the 84 mathematics items included in the mathematics section of PISA 2003. The observed responses are both dichotomous and polytomous. Student characteristics, such as home language, gender, and social class, may influence student achievement levels; and they are included as potentially construct-irrelevant sources of variation in the model.

The following partial credit model illustrates the main effects of our conceptual model:

$$Ln \left[\frac{P_{nijmpki1}}{P_{nijmpki0}} \right] \theta_n - \delta_i - \alpha_j - \lambda_m - \gamma_p - \tau_{ki} \qquad [1]$$

where

$P_{nijmpki1}$ = the probability of person n succeeding on item *i* for group *j*, group *m*, group *p*, and threshold *k*,

$P_{nijmpki0}$ = the probability of person *n* failing on item *i* for group *j*, group *m*, group *p*, and threshold *k*,

θ_n = the location of person *n* on the latent variable,

---

4 Note that the FACETS software uses joint maximum likelihood estimation. This estimation method is known to produce bias in parameter estimates (Andersen, 1972; Haberman, 1977). We applied the appropriate bias correction available in FACETS when conducting our analyses.

Figure 2: Conceptual model

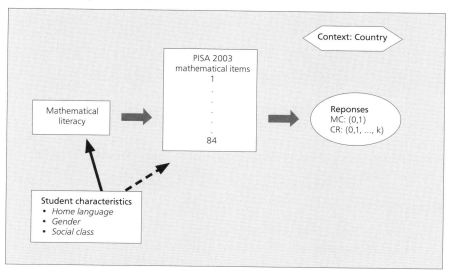

δ_i = the difficulty of item i,

α_j = the location of language group j,

λ_m = the location of gender group m,

γ_p = the location of social class group p, and

τ_{ki} = the kth threshold parameter of item i.

We examined main effects for the five facets—students, test items, home language, gender, and social class—across the four countries of interest. We subsequently used the main effects model to generate fit statistics, infit mean-square and outfit mean-square, as well as reliability of separation and chi-square statistics.

Infit mean-square and outfit mean-square are fit statistics that quantify the degree to which items or persons deviate from the expected model. The infit statistic is the sum of the squared-standardized residuals (Z^2_{ni}) summed over each element within a facet. This variance is then averaged by dividing it by the number of items the individual responded to, after which it is weighted by the individual's variance (W_{ni}) to account for the impact of the outliers, resulting in an infit statistic of the type seen in Equation 2 (Bond & Fox, 2007; Petridou & Williams, 2007). For this reason, infit is referred to as the information-weighted sum.

$$Inf\ it = \frac{\Sigma\ Z_{ni}^2 W_{ni}}{\Sigma W_{ni}} \quad [2]$$

The outfit statistic is calculated similarly, as seen in Equation 3. The difference between the infit and outfit statistics lies in the fact that the residuals are not weighted.

$$Ontf\ it = \frac{\Sigma\ Z_{ni}^2}{N} \quad [3]$$

Item difficulties were anchored at the actual item difficulties used in PISA 2003, based on the total number of participating countries. The student facet was not centered at zero. The other facets in the model were centered at zero (similar to contrast coding in multiple regression analyses) to estimate the contrasts between the elements within each facet.

RESULTS

As is apparent in Table 2, the reliability of separation for the items signifies that the PISA 2003 mathematics items included in our study manifested an array of difficulties. The chi-square statistic for the students and mathematics test items showed that the mean differences in students' mathematical literacy were statistically significant at the 0.05 level. Reliability of separation for gender and social class ranged from 0.63 to 0.89 across the countries. Gender and social class mean differences were also statistically significant in each of the four countries, except France, where gender had no statistically significant influence on mathematical literacy. The language facet had a statistically significant influence on mathematical literacy in all countries.

Figures 3 through 6 present the empirical variable maps for each country in the study. Each variable map displays the location of the five facets on the same scale of measurement. For example, Figure 3 shows that the male and female students sampled in France have the same location on the latent variable mathematical literacy. However, Figure 5 shows that male and female students sampled in Hong Kong have different locations on mathematical literacy, with females having a higher location on the latent variable. Readers should be cautioned that these are very small differences on the logit scale; one rule of thumb suggests differences less than 0.30 logits may not have substantive significance.

The variable maps also show a wide spread of item difficulties within each country. The percent of variance collectively explained by the five facets in the model is high at 76.9% in France, 76.0% in Germany, 79.1% in Hong Kong, and 74.5% in the United States. These are quite good degrees of model-data fit, and they provide support for the inference that the test is unidimensional.

The expected value of the mean-square error statistics (infit and outfit) was 1.00, with a standard deviation of 0.20. The infit statistics for the facets across countries were all within the expected range of 0.80 to 1.20. However, the standard deviation of the infit for students was somewhat higher than expected, a finding that may reflect individual differences. This finding prompts additional explorations of person fit.

Table 2: Summary of FACETS statistics main effects

	France					Germany				
	Students	Items	Language	Gender	Class	Students	Items	Language	Gender	Class
Measures										
M	0.44	-0.01	0.00	0.00	0.00	0.42	0.18	0.00	0.00	0.00
SD	1.15	1.15	0.06	0.03	0.08	0.70	1.09	0.09	0.03	0.09
N	1,000	84	2	2	4	1,000	84	2	2	4
Infit										
M	1.05	1.02	1.07	1.08	1.09	1.05	1.05	1.14	1.09	1.10
SD	526	0.19	1.14	0.01	0.02	0.48	0.28	0.06	0.01	0.03
Outfit										
M	1.1	1.14	1.14	1.16	1.24	1.07	1.09	1.26	1.08	1.17
SD	0.94	1.0	1.49	0.01	0.15	0.86	0.72	0.22	0.22	
Reliability of separation		0.98	0.75	0.63	0.87		0.98	0.89	0.70	0.89
Chi-square statistic		6010*	8.0*	5.50	54.2*		1420.4*	18.5*	6.6*	54.5*
Degrees of freedom		83	1	1	3		83	1	1	3

	Hong Kong					United States				
	Students	Items	Language	Gender	Class	Students	Items	Language	Gender	Class
Measures										
M	0.68	-0.01	0.00	0.00	0.00	-0.09	0.00	0.00	0.00	0.00
SD	0.76	1.07	0.08	0.03	0.05	1.13	1.07	0.05	0.03	0.09
N	1,000	84	2	2	4	1,000	84	2	2	4
Infit										
M	1.01	1.01	1.05	1.06	1.06	1.09	1.02	1.11	1.10	1.11
SD	0.49	0.18	0.03	0.01	0.02	0.46	0.24	0.01	0.01	0.02
Outfit										
M	1.10	1.12	1.31	1.18	1.18	1.05	1.04	1.08	1.05	1.08
SD	1.09	0.99	0.16	0.03	0.12	0.59	0.47	0.03	0.01	0.04
Reliability of separation		0.98	0.89	0.77	0.77		0.99	0.74	0.77	0.89
Chi-square statistic		6536.5*	17.6*	8.7*	18.4*		6725.1*	7.6*	8.9*	66.7*
Degrees of freedom		83	1	1	3		83	1	1	3

Note: $*p < .05$.

Figure 3: Empirical variable map for France

```
+--------------------------------------------------------------------------------+
|Measr|+Student    |-Item                             |+Gender|+Lang |+Class      |
|-----+------------+----------------------------------+-------+------+------------|
|  5 + .           +                                  +       +      +            |
|     |            |                                  |       |      |            |
|     |            |                                  |       |      |            |
|     |            |                                  |       |      |            |
|  4 + +           +                                  +       +      +            |
|     |            |                                  |       |      |            |
|     |            |                                  |       |      |            |
|     |            | 45                               |       |      |            |
|  3 + .           +                                  +       +      +            |
|     |            |                                  |       |      |            |
|     |    .       |                                  |       |      |            |
|     |    .       | 40                               |       |      |            |
|     |    .       |                                  |       |      |            |
|  2 + *.          +                                  +       +      +            |
|     |    *.      | 76                               |       |      |            |
|     |    **.     | 6   7  15  47                    |       |      |            |
|     |    ****.   | 23  48  80                       |       |      |            |
|     |    ******. | 4   17  18  29  73               |       |      |            |
|  1 + ********.   + 26  27  28                       +       +      +            |
|     |  ********. | 39  66                           |       |      |            |
|     | *********. | 2   55  74  83                   |       |      |            |
|     | *********. | 3   8   12  50  56  58           |       |      |            |
|     | *********. | 5   9   24  32  35  43  49  60  65  71  81 |   | WC High     |
| *  0 * ********. * 20  25  31  38  42  57  77  82    * F   M  * N  Y * BC High  BC Low    WC Low  *
|     |   ******.  | 14  64  70                       |       |      |            |
|     |   *****    | 11  19  52  59  67  78           |       |      |            |
|     |   **.      | 13  44  54  61  84               |       |      |            |
|     |    *.      | 30  53  63  68  69  72           |       |      |            |
| -1 + .           + 10  36  37  46  51  79           +       +      +            |
|     |    .       |                                  |       |      |            |
|     |    .       | 1   16  22                       |       |      |            |
|     |    .       | 75                               |       |      |            |
| -2 + .           + 34  62                           +       +      +            |
|     |    .       |                                  |       |      |            |
|     |    .       | 33                               |       |      |            |
|     |    .       | 41                               |       |      |            |
|     |    .       |                                  |       |      |            |
| -3 + .           +                                  +       +      +            |
|     |    .       |                                  |       |      |            |
|     |            |                                  |       |      |            |
|     |    .       |                                  |       |      |            |
| -4 + .           +                                  +       +      +            |
|     |            |                                  |       |      |            |
|     |            | 21                               |       |      |            |
|     |            |                                  |       |      |            |
| -5 + .           +                                  +       +      +            |
|-----+------------+----------------------------------+-------+------+------------|
|Measr| * = 44     |-Item                             |+Gender|+Lang |+Class      |
+--------------------------------------------------------------------------------+
```

The outfit statistics for the facets across the countries were within the expected range, with the exception of the language facet. In both France and the United States, these values were higher than expected based on the model. The standard deviations of the outfit statistics were also high for the student and item facets across the countries.

Figure 7 shows the results of our exploration of group response functions. Here we can see the functional relationships between the probability of a correct response and the location of students within the two language groups. We used the location of the language groups—students who spoke the language of the test at home and students who did not speak the language of the test at home—along with the discrimination (slope) parameters to construct the group response functions for each country. Even though we found statistically significant differences for all countries, these displays

Figure 4: Empirical variable map for Germany

```
+-------------------------------------------------------------------------+
|Measr|+Student    |-Item                      |+Gender|+Lang |+Class      |
|-----+------------+---------------------------+-------+------+------------|
|   5 + .          +                           +       +      +            |
|     |            |                           |       |      |            |
|     |            |                           |       |      |            |
|     |     .      |                           |       |      |            |
|   4 +            +                           +       +      +            |
|     |            |                           |       |      |            |
|     |            |                           |       |      |            |
|     |     .      |                           |       |      |            |
|     |            |                           |       |      |            |
|   3 + .          + 45                         +       +      +            |
|     |            |                           |       |      |            |
|     |     .      |                           |       |      |            |
|     |     .      | 40                         |       |      |            |
|   2 + .          +                           +       +      +            |
|     |     *.     | 29 47                      |       |      |            |
|     |     *.     | 15 80                      |       |      |            |
|     |     ***.   | 6  28 73 76                |       |      |            |
|     |     ****.  | 4  7  17 23 27 66          |       |      |            |
|   1 + ******.    + 26 48 58                   +       +      +            |
|     | ********.  | 18 39 71 81 83             |       |      |            |
|     | ********.  | 2  49 57 74                |       |      |            |
|     | *********. | 8  35 43 65                |       |      |            |
|     | *********. | 3  9  12 24 31 32 56 60    |       |      | WC High    |
| *   0 * ********. * 25 38 42 50 70            * F  M  * N  Y * BC High  WC Low  *
|     | *******.   | 14 20 44 55 64 77          |       |      | BC Low     |
|     | ****.      | 5  19 61 67 68 82 84       |       |      |            |
|     | ***        | 11 52 59                   |       |      |            |
|     | *.         | 10 13 30 37 46 54 63       |       |      |            |
|  -1 + *.         + 22 78                      +       +      +            |
|     | .          | 16 36 51 53 69 72 75       |       |      |            |
|     | .          | 1                          |       |      |            |
|     | .          | 79                         |       |      |            |
|     | .          |                            |       |      |            |
|  -2 + .          + 33 34                      +       +      +            |
|     | .          | 41                         |       |      |            |
|     |            | 62                         |       |      |            |
|     |            |                            |       |      |            |
|     | .          |                            |       |      |            |
|  -3 +            +                            +       +      +            |
|     |            |                            |       |      |            |
|     |            |                            |       |      |            |
|     |            |                            |       |      |            |
|     |            |                            |       |      |            |
|  -4 +            + 21                         +       +      +            |
|     |            |                            |       |      |            |
|     |            |                            |       |      |            |
|     |            |                            |       |      |            |
|     |            |                            |       |      |            |
|  -5 + .          +                            +       +      +            |
|-----+------------+----------------------------+-------+------+------------|
|Measr| * = 46     |-Item                       |+Gender|+Lang |+Class      |
+-------------------------------------------------------------------------+
```

highlight the small substantive impact of these differences. Despite the overlap of language groups shown in Figure 7, there are still students within each group who exhibit unexpected response patterns.

Figure 5: Empirical variable map for Hong Kong

```
+--------------------------------------------------------------------------------+
|Measr|+Student    |-Item                 |+Gender|+Lang |+Class                  |
|-----+------------+--------------------------------+------+------+-----------------|
|  5 + .           +                      |      +      +      +                   |
|     |            |                      |      |      |      |                   |
|     |            |                      |      |      |      |                   |
|     |  .         |                      |      |      |      |                   |
|  4 +            +                       |      +      +      +                   |
|     |            |                      |      |      |      |                   |
|     |  .         |                      |      |      |      |                   |
|     |  .         |                      |      |      |      |                   |
|  3 + .          +                       |      +      +      +                   |
|     |  .         |                      |      |      |      |                   |
|     |  .         | 7  40                |      |      |      |                   |
|     |  .         | 45                   |      |      |      |                   |
|     | *.         |                      |      |      |      |                   |
|  2 + **.        +                       |      +      +      +                   |
|     | ***.       | 47                   |      |      |      |                   |
|     | ****.      | 26 76                |      |      |      |                   |
|     | *******.   | 15 29                |      |      |      |                   |
|     | *******.   | 23 66 80             |      |      |      |                   |
|  1 + ********.  + 6  17 39 73 83        |      +      +      +                   |
|     | ********.  | 4  10 12 25 28 57    |      |      |      |                   |
|     | ********.  | 2  9  18 48 49 65 71 74 |   |      |      |                   |
|     | ********.  | 8  27 35 56          |      |      |      |                   |
|     | ********.  | 20 24 31 32 43 70 84 |      |      |      |                   |
|  * * 0 * *******. * 38 60 67 81         | * F  M * N  Y * BC High  BC Low    WC High  WC Low *
|     | *****.     | 42 51 55 82          |      |      |      |                   |
|     | ***.       | 3  11 19 58 59 64    |      |      |      |                   |
|     | **.        | 14 44 52 61          |      |      |      |                   |
|     | *.         | 13 30 41 46 54 63    |      |      |      |                   |
| -1 + .          + 50 53 68 69 78        |      +      +      +                   |
|     | .          | 1  5  22 75 77 79    |      |      |      |                   |
|     | .          | 36 37                |      |      |      |                   |
|     | .          | 16                   |      |      |      |                   |
|     | .          | 34 62 72             |      |      |      |                   |
| -2 + .          + 33                    |      +      +      +                   |
|     | .          |                      |      |      |      |                   |
|     |            |                      |      |      |      |                   |
|     |            |                      |      |      |      |                   |
| -3 +            +                       |      +      +      +                   |
|     |            | 21                   |      |      |      |                   |
|     |            |                      |      |      |      |                   |
|     |            |                      |      |      |      |                   |
| -4 +            +                       |      +      +      +                   |
|     |            |                      |      |      |      |                   |
|     |            |                      |      |      |      |                   |
|     |            |                      |      |      |      |                   |
| -5 + .          +                       |      +      +      +                   |
|-----+------------+--------------------------------+------+------+-----------------|
|Measr| * = 44     |-Item                 |+Gender|+Lang |+Class                  |
+--------------------------------------------------------------------------------+
```

Figure 6: Empirical variable map for the United States

```
+------------------------------------------------------------------------------------+
|Measr|+Student    |-Item                      |+Gender|+Lang |+Class                 |
|-----+------------+---------------------------+-------+------+-----------------------|
|  5 + .          +                           +       +      +                        |
|    |            |                           |       |      |                        |
|    |            |                           |       |      |                        |
|    |            |                           |       |      |                        |
|    |            |                           |       |      |                        |
|  4 +            +                           +       +      +                        |
|    |            |                           |       |      |                        |
|    |            |                           |       |      |                        |
|    |            |                           |       |      |                        |
|  3 + .          + 45                        +       +      +                        |
|    | .          |                           |       |      |                        |
|    | .          | 40                        |       |      |                        |
|    | .          |                           |       |      |                        |
|    | .          |                           |       |      |                        |
|  2 + .          +                           +       +      +                        |
|    | .          | 28 29 80                  |       |      |                        |
|    | .          | 4  15 27 48 55            |       |      |                        |
|    | *.         | 47 73                     |       |      |                        |
|    | *.         | 6  26 76                  |       |      |                        |
|  1 + **.        + 7  23                     +       +      +                        |
|    | ****.      | 2  17 18 83               |       |      |                        |
|    | ****.      | 8  39 41 66 81            |       |      |                        |
|    | ******.    | 25 35 43 70 71            |       |      |                        |
|    | ********.  | 49 56 57 58               |       |      | WC High              |
| *  0 * *********.* 3  9  10 20 31 74 82     * F  M * N  Y * BC High  BC Low  WC Low *
|    | *********. | 5  12 32 42 44 65         |       |      |                        |
|    | *********. | 11 24 33 38 60 67 84      |       |      |                        |
|    | *******.   | 14 50 52 54 59 64 77      |       |      |                        |
|    | *****.     | 13 19 37 51 61 68 75 79   |       |      |                        |
| -1 + ***.       + 30 34 78                  +       +      +                        |
|    | **.        | 46 53 63 69               |       |      |                        |
|    | *          | 22 72                     |       |      |                        |
|    | .          | 1  36                     |       |      |                        |
|    | .          | 16 62                     |       |      |                        |
| -2 + .          +                           +       +      +                        |
|    | .          |                           |       |      |                        |
|    | .          |                           |       |      |                        |
|    | .          |                           |       |      |                        |
|    | .          |                           |       |      |                        |
| -3 +            +                           +       +      +                        |
|    | .          |                           |       |      |                        |
|    | .          | 21                        |       |      |                        |
|    |            |                           |       |      |                        |
|    |            |                           |       |      |                        |
| -4 +            +                           +       +      +                        |
|    |            |                           |       |      |                        |
|    |            |                           |       |      |                        |
|    |            |                           |       |      |                        |
|    |            |                           |       |      |                        |
| -5 + .          +                           +       +      +                        |
|-----+------------+---------------------------+-------+------+-----------------------|
|Measr| * = 61     |-Item                      |+Gender|+Lang |+Class                 |
+------------------------------------------------------------------------------------+
```

Figure 7: Language group response functions

	France		Germany		Hong Kong		United States	
	Lang (N)	*Lang (Y)*	*Lang (N)*	*Lang (Y)*	*Lang (N)*	*Lang (Y)*	*Lang (N)*	*Lang (Y)*
Location	-0.06	0.06	-0.09	0.09	-0.08	0.08	-0.05	0.05
Discrimination	0.81	0.99	0.78	1.00	0.86	1.01	0.90	0.97˙
Infit MNSQ	1.14	1.07	1.21	1.08	1.11	1.05	1.12	1.10
Outfit MNSQ	1.49	1.14	1.48	1.05	1.48	1.15	1.13	9.00

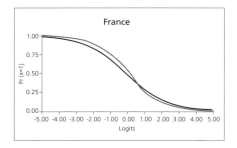

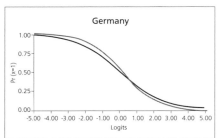

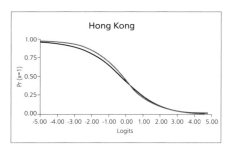

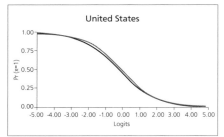

Note: All of the differences between language groups are statistically significant within countries ($p < .05$).

In order to illustrate these unexpected response patterns at the level of the individual, we chose three students from each language group in France and Germany; Figures 8 and 9 show the functional relationships for these individual-level student responses. The students we chose from each of these two countries had identical overall test scores (38 in France and 54 in Germany). In each language group, we identified a student in one of three fit classifications: less variation than expected (Persons A/D), fit the model (Persons B/E), did not fit the model (Persons C/F). Despite the statistically significant influence of the language facet, observations of the PRFs showed unexpected response patterns for certain students. The relationship between outfit and discrimination is also illustrated in the two figures. The correlation between these two student measures was fairly high at -0.649 in France and -0.711 in Germany.

Figure 8: Illustration of person response functions in France

	Language of test (Yes)			Language of test (No)		
	Person A	Person B	Person C	Person D	Person E	Person F
Location	-0.01	1.17	0.57	1.25	1.22	-0.25
Discrimination	1.60	0.42	-0.13	1.01	0.85	0.26
Infit MNSQ	0.48	2.26	1.59	0.41	0.67	1.47
Outfit MNSQ	0.48	1.18	1.63	0.39	1.06	1.52

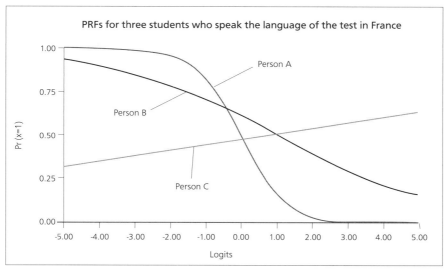

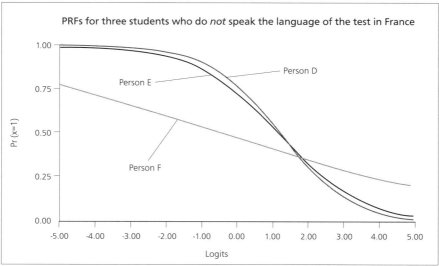

Figure 9: Illustration of person response functions in Germany

	Language of test (Yes)			Language of test (No)		
	Person A	Person B	Person C	Person D	Person E	Person F
Location	-0.18	0.35	0.50	0.60	0.05	0.76
Discrimination	1.12	0.64	0.40	1.42	0.54	0.51
Infit MNSQ	0.35	1.32	1.27	0.72	1.07	1.47
Outf i MNSQ	0.57	1.15	1.88	0.56	1.18	1.83

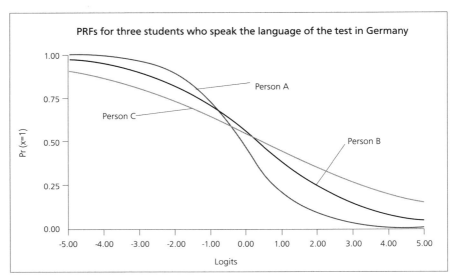

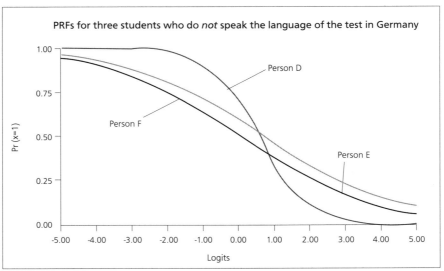

DISCUSSION

The focus of our study was exploration of the relationships between mathematical literacy and several student characteristics. Rasch measurement theory provided the methodological framework for conducting our analyses, which meant we could look at item-level rather than simply score-level information about students. Our analyses showed a relationship between home language and mathematics literacy within each of the four countries from which we drew samples of students who participated in PISA 2003 (i.e., France, Germany, Hong Kong, and the United States).

We found that gender and social class had significant influences on students' mathematics literacy in Germany, Hong Kong, and the United States, but not in France. Although we describe results in this paper as statistically significant, we do so with a caveat. The FACETS software that we used applies joint maximum likelihood (JML) estimation, which is known to produce biased parameter estimates (Andersen, 1972; Haberman, 1977). Although we applied the approximate bias correction available in FACETS to the analyses presented here, and although item difficulties were anchored on the actual values used in the PISA 2003 study, thus reducing the effects of using JML, we cannot be assured that the results reported as significant would be confirmed in a reanalysis using an unbiased estimation method.

The findings reported here are consistent with the findings of other recent research. Within an international context, gender differences in students' mathematics literacy continue to be salient across some countries. As we stated earlier, 28 out of the 41 PISA 2003 countries reported significant score-level gender differences (OECD, 2004). Social class, which we included in this study by using the students' parental occupation, is also a well-known predictor of achievement (OECD, 2006).

The use of group and person response functions offers a promising approach for examining aspects of student performance related to mathematical literacy on the PISA 2003 test items. The group response functions for language groups indicated that, despite the overall statistically significant effects for all countries, the small distances between the group response functions may not be substantively important. However, we still found significant individual differences in response patterns that may limit the inferences regarding mathematical literacy for some students. Figures 8 and 9 illustrate this phenomenon.

It is important to consider certain limitations that can also serve as recommendations for future research in the area of mathematics literacy. First of all, this study was a secondary data analysis. We had no direct control over the design of the assessment or decisions made with respect to the sampling design. As Rutkowski et al. (2010) point out, sampling weights should be used in order to adequately represent student achievement in each country. We used senate weights in our study to explore both national and individual levels of performance by students on each item representing mathematical literacy. Secondly, even though the main effects were statistically significant, the actual effect sizes on the logit scale were quite small. Because these small differences may not have any substantive significance, we again caution readers against over-interpreting these main effects. Finally, there is a need to recognize the significant individual differences within each of the student subgroups examined here.

CONCLUSION

In summary, the results of this study on the influences of home language, gender, and social class on mathematical literacy confirm previous research that each of these factors is related to mathematical literacy. Our use of Rasch measurement provided results consistent with earlier findings based on PISA 2003. The study also illustrated how group and person response functions can be used to explore student response on mathematics items at a micro-level of analysis.

References

Andersen E. B. (1972). The numerical solution of a set of conditional estimation equations. *Journal of the Royal Statistical Society*, Series B, *34*, 42–54.

Beeghley, L. (2004). *The structure of social stratification in the United State*s. Boston, MA: Pearson, Allyn & Bacon.

Bond, T. G, & Fox, C. M. (2007). *Applying the Rasch model: Fundamental measurement in the human sciences* (2nd ed.). Mahwah, NJ: Lawrence Erlbaum Associates.

Carey, D. (2008). Improving education outcomes in Germany. *OECD Economics Department Working Papers, No. 611*. Paris, France: OECD Publications.

Carroll, J. B. (1983). Psychometric theory and language testing. In J. W. Oller, Jr. (Ed.), *Issues in language testing research* (pp. 80–107). Rowley, MA: Newbury House Publishers.

Carroll, J. M. (2007). *A concise history of Hong Kong*. Lanham, MD: Rowman & Littlefield.

Castles, S. (2004). Migration, citizenship, and education. In J. A. Banks (Ed.), *Diversity and citizenship education: Global perspectives* (pp. 17–48). San Francisco, CA: Jossey-Bass.

Castles, S., & Miller, M. J. (2003). *The age of migration: International population movements in the modern world* (3rd ed.). New York, NY: Guilford.

Else-Quest, N., Hyde, J., & Linn, M. (2010). Cross-national patterns of gender differences in mathematics: A meta-analysis. *Psychological Bulletin, 136*, 103–127.

Engelhard, G. (in press). *Invariant measurement: Using Rasch models in the social, behavioral, and health science*s. New York, NY: Routledge.

Ganzeboom, H. B. G., & Treiman, D. J. (1996). Internationally comparable measures of occupational status for the 1988 International Standard Classification of Occupations. *Social Science Research, 25*, 201–239.

Haberman S. J. (1977). Maximum likelihood estimates in exponential response models. *The Annals of Statistics, 5*, 815–841.

Keats, J. A. (1967). Test theory. *Annual Review of Psychology, 18*, 217–238.

Legislative Council. (2007). *Analysis of income disparity in Hong Kong*. Hong Kong, SAR: Legislative Council. Retrieved from http://www.legco.gov.hk/yr06-07/english/fc/fc/papers/fc0301fc-46-e.pdf

Levine, M. V., & Rubin, D. B. (1979). Measuring the appropriateness of multiple-choice test scores. *Journal of Educational Statistics, 4*, 269–290.

Linacre, J. M. (2010). *FACETS* (Version 3) [Computer program]. Chicago, IL: MESA Press.

Liu, O., & Wilson, M. (2009a). Gender differences in large-scale math assessments: PISA trends 2000 and 2003. *Applied Measurement in Education, 22*(2), 164–184.

Liu, O., & Wilson, M. (2009b). Gender differences and similarities in PISA 2003 mathematics: A comparison between the United States and Hong Kong. *International Journal of Testing, 9*(1), 20–40.

Lumsden, J. (1977). Person reliability. *Applied Psychological Measurement, 1*(4), 477–482.

Lumsden, J. (1980). Variations on a theme by Thurstone. *Applied Psychological Measurement, 4*(1), 1–7.

Marks, G. (2006). Are between- and within-school differences in student performance largely due to socio-economic background? Evidence from 30 countries. *Educational Research, 48*(1), 21–40.

Miller, D. C., Sen, A., & Malley, L. B. (2007). *Comparative indicators of education in the United States and other G8 countries: 2006*. Retrieved from http://www.nces.ed.gov

Mosier, C. I. (1940). Psychophysics and mental test theory: Fundamental postulates and elementary theorems. *Psychological Review, 47*, 355–366.

Mosier, C. I. (1941). Psychophysics and mental test theory. II. The constant process. *Psychological Review, 48*, 235–249.

Mullis, I., Martin, M., Gonzalez, E., & Chrostowski, S. (2004). *TIMSS 2003 international mathematics report: Findings from IEA's Trends in International Mathematics and Science Study at the fourth and eighth grades*. Chestnut Hill, MA: Boston College.

Organisation for Economic Co-operation and Development (OECD). (2003). *The PISA 2003 assessment framework*. Paris, France: OECD Publications.

Organisation for Economic Co-operation and Development (OECD). (2004). *Learning for tomorrow's world: First results from PISA 2003*. Paris, France: OECD Publications.

Organisation for Economic Co-operation and Development (OECD). (2006). *Where immigrant students succeed: A comparative review of performance and engagement in PISA 2003*. Paris, France: OECD Publications.

Perkins, A., & Engelhard, G. (2009). Crossing person response functions. *Rasch Measurement Transactions, 23*(1), 1183–1184.

Petridou, A., & Williams, J. (2007). Accounting for aberrant test response patterns using multilevel models. *Journal of Educational Measurement, 44*(3), 227–247.

Rasch, G. (1980). *Probabilistic models for some intelligence and attainment tests* (expanded edition). Chicago, IL: University of Chicago Press (Original work published 1960).

Robertson, I. (2005). Issues relating to curriculum, policy and gender raised by national and international surveys of achievement in mathematics. *Assessment in Education: Principles, Policy and Practice*, *12*(3), 217–236.

Rolka, K. (2004). Bilingual lessons and mathematical world views: A German perspective. In M. J. Hoines & A. B. Fuglestad (Eds.), *Proceedings of the 28th Conference of the International Group for the Psychology of Mathematics Education* (pp. 105–112). Cape Town, South Africa: International Group for the Psychology of Mathematics Education.

Rutkowski, L., Gonzalez, E., Joncas, M., & von Davier, M. (2010). International large-scale assessment data: Issues in secondary analysis and reporting. *Educational Researcher*, *39*(2), 142–151.

Salaff, J., & Siu-Lun, W. (1995). Exiting Hong Kong: Social class experiences and the adjustment to 1997. In Ronald Skeldon (Ed.), *Emigration from Hong Kong: Trends and tendencies* (pp. 179–211). Hong Kong, SAR: Chinese University Press.

Thompson, W., & Hickey, J. (2005). *Society in focus*. Boston, MA: Pearson, Allyn & Bacon.

Turner, R., & Adams, R. J. (2007). The Programme for International Student Assessment: An overview. *Journal of Applied Measurement*, *8*(3), 237–248.

Vale, C. D., & Weiss, D. J. (1975). *A study of computer-administered adaptive testing* (Report 75-4, NTIS No. Ad-A018758). Minneapolis, MN: Psychometric Methods Program, Department of Psychology, University of Minnesota.

van Langen, A., Bosker, R., & Dekkers, H. (2006). Exploring cross-national differences in gender gaps in education. *Educational Research and Evaluation*, *12*(2), 155–177.

Weiss, D. J. (1973). *The stratified adaptive computerized ability test* (Report 73-3, NTIS No. AD-768376). Minneapolis, MN: Psychometric Methods Program, Department of Psychology, University of Minnesota.

Hierarchical factor item response theory models for PIRLS: capturing clustering effects at multiple levels[1]

Frank Rijmen
Educational Testing Service, Princeton, New Jersey, USA

In large-scale assessments, items are often clustered at multiple levels. For example, the Progress in International Reading Literacy Study (PIRLS) assessment consists of item blocks. Each item block contains a reading passage followed by a set of questions. In turn, blocks of items are clustered within a literary versus an informational reading purpose. An alternative item classification scheme that is crossed with item blocks is based on the comprehension process that is involved in each of the items. The conditional dependencies between items of the same cluster can be taken into account by incorporating cluster-specific dimensions in addition to a general dimension representing overall reading ability, resulting in either a higher-order or a hierarchical model. Both types of models are formulated and applied to the PIRLS 2006 assessment. In addition, a hierarchical model is presented that incorporates a multidimensional general structure. Results indicated a moderate effect of item blocks in addition to a predominantly unidimensional general structure.

---

1   The research reported here was supported by the Institute of Education Sciences, U.S. Department of Education, through grant R305D110027 to Educational Testing Service. The opinions expressed are those of the author and do not represent the views of Educational Testing Service, the Institute of Education Sciences, or the U.S. Department of Education.

INTRODUCTION

The Progress in International Reading Literacy Study (PIRLS) is an internationally comparative reading assessment that has been carried out every five years since its inception in 2001. In 2006, there were 40 participating countries, totaling more than 200,000 participants. The study is aimed at measuring trends in children's reading literacy achievement (TIMSS & PIRLS International Study Center, Boston College, 2010).

Two overarching purposes of reading are assessed in PIRLS: (a) reading to acquire and use information, and (b) reading for literary experience. In literary reading, "... the reader engages with the text to become involved in imagined events, settings, actions, consequences, characters, atmosphere, feelings, and ideas, and to enjoy language itself" (Mullis, Kennedy, Martin, & Sainsbury, 2006, p. 19). In contrast, when reading for information, "...the reader engages not with imagined worlds, but with aspects of the real universe" (Mullis et al., 2006, p. 9). Each purpose is assessed through a set of questions that are clustered within text materials.

Another aspect of reading literacy that PIRLS focuses on is comprehension. The study distinguishes among four comprehension processes (Mullis et al., 2006): focus on and retrieve explicitly stated information, make straightforward inferences, interpret and integrate ideas and information, and examine and evaluate content, language, and textual elements. Every item assesses a single comprehension process. Each block of items assesses all four comprehension processes.

Taken together, items cluster both within reading purposes and within comprehension processes. Reading purposes are crossed with comprehension processes. Furthermore, item blocks corresponding to test materials are nested within reading purposes, and crossed with comprehension processes. Finally, the cross-classification of items is not completely balanced: the proportions of items measuring the four comprehension processes are not constant across item blocks or reading purposes.

PIRLS reports a scale for overall reading literacy as well as separate scales for purposes of reading and for comprehension processes. As might be assumed, there are two scales for reading purposes. However, there are only two scales for comprehension processes, despite four processes being identified. The first of these two scales combines the first two processes listed above; the second combines the latter two. Item parameters are calibrated separately for each of the five scales using a unidimensional item response theory model. The psychometric analyses used in PIRLS currently do not take into account the clustering of items within item blocks.

In this paper, I will present a set of multidimensional item response theory models that do take into account the effects of item clustering within item blocks and reading purposes, on the one hand, and within comprehension processes, on the other. The use of multidimensional item response theory models has always been hampered by the computational burden to obtain maximum likelihood parameter estimates, a difficulty that is amplified by the sheer size of large-scale assessment datasets.

However, if one is willing to assume specific conditional independence relations between the different dimensions of the model, exact maximum likelihood estimation methods can often be applied, even for a large number of dimensions (Rijmen, 2009, 2010, in press; Rijmen, Vansteelandt, & De Boeck, 2008). I begin my account by describing various multidimensional item response theory models, starting with the simpler and better-known models and moving to the more complex.

MULTIDIMENSIONAL ITEM RESPONSE MODELS

Hierarchical Models

The best-known example of a hierarchical model is the bifactor model. The bifactor model first appeared in the factor analysis literature for continuous manifest variables (Holzinger & Swineford, 1937). Gibbons and Hedeker (1992) adapted the model for binary data. In the bifactor model, each item is an indicator of a general dimension and one of K other dimensions. The general dimension stands for the latent variable of central interest (i.e., reading literacy), whereas the K other dimensions are incorporated to take into account additional dependencies between items belonging to the same cluster (i.e., item block, reading purpose, comprehension process).

For binary data, the bifactor model can be defined as follows. Let $\mathbf{y}_{j(k)}$ denote the binary scored response on the jth item, $j = 1,...., J$, embedded within testlet k, $k = 1,..., K$. There are J_k items embedded within each item cluster k, hence $\sum_{k=1}^{K} J_k = J$. The response vector pertaining to item cluster k is denoted by $\mathbf{y}_k$, and the vector of all responses is denoted by $\mathbf{y}$. Conditional on K cluster-specific latent variables θ_k and a general latent variable θ_g that is common to all items, statistical independent is assumed between all responses. Thus:

$$P(\mathbf{y}|\boldsymbol{\theta}) = \prod_{j=1}^{J} P(\mathbf{y}_{j(k)}|\theta_g, \theta_k), \qquad (1)$$

where $\boldsymbol{\theta} = (\theta_g, \theta_{1,...}, \theta_{k,...}, \theta_K)$.

Typically, the latent variables are assumed to be uncorrelated and normally distributed. Figure 1 presents the directed acyclic graph of the bifactor model with uncorrelated latent variables. In the figure, arrows represent conditional dependence relations. The graph represents a model with four item blocks. Items that belong to the same item block are represented by a single node because they depend on the same set of latent variables.

Figure 1: Directed acyclic graph of a bifactor model

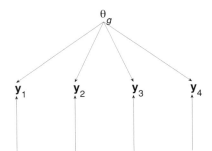

Furthermore, $\pi_j = P(y_{j(k)} = 1 | \theta_g, \theta_k)$ is related to a linear function of the latent variables through a link function $g(\cdot)$,

$$g(\pi_j) = \alpha_{jg}\theta_g + \alpha_{jk}\theta_k + \beta_j , \qquad (2)$$

where $g(\cdot)$ is typically the probit or logit link function. The parameter β_j is the intercept parameter for item j, and α_{jg} and α_{jk} are the slopes or loadings of item j on the general and specific latent variables. Note that several distinct but formally equivalent parameterizations are in use in the item response theory and factor analysis literature for the model presented in Equation 2.

When the slope parameters α_{jg} and α_{jk} are known constants, a one-parameter bifactor model is obtained. Alternatively, an item-guessing parameter can also be incorporated into the expressions for the π_j's. Furthermore, for polytomous responses, the model can be extended in a straightforward way by choosing a link function $g(\cdot)$ for polytomous data (Fahrmeir & Tutz, 2001).

In order to identify the model, the location and the scale of all dimensions are fixed. Typically, the mean and variance of each dimension is set to zero and one, respectively, so that, under the assumption of normally distributed latent variables, $\theta \sim N(\mathbf{0}, \mathbf{I})$.

In this paper, the logit link function is used for binary items, $g(\pi_j) = \log(\pi_j/(1 - \pi_j))$. For polytomous items, the cumulative link functions is incorporated, $g(\pi_j^{c+}) = \log(\pi_j^{c+}/(1 - \pi_j^{c+}))$, with c denoting the response category, and $\pi_j^{c+} = P(y_{j(k)c} > c | \theta_g, \theta_k)$ for $c = 0, ..., C_j - 1$.

The bifactor model does not suffer from the problem of dimensionality that other multidimensional item response theory models do with respect to maximum likelihood parameter estimation. The reason is that the bifactor structure can be exploited when the expectation step of the expectation maximization (EM) algorithm is carried out. Specifically, the integration over all $K+1$ latent variables can be carried out through a sequence of computations in two-dimensional subspaces, where each subspace consists of the general dimension and one specific dimension. Gibbons and Hedeker

(1992) proved this result under the conditions of normally and independently distributed latent variables, and for the probit link. These limiting conditions were due to the fact that the authors relied on properties of the multivariate normal distribution.

Recently, Rijmen (2009, 2010) showed that the result is a specific example of a general procedure to exploit conditional independence relations during parameter estimation. The procedure is embedded within a graphical model framework for latent variable models (Rijmen, in press; Rijmen et al., 2008). Rijmen (2009) showed that the conditions of independently distributed latent variables can be relaxed to conditional independence of the specific dimensions, given the general dimension. Furthermore, because one does not have to rely on properties of the normal distribution, the result remains valid under any link function other than the probit function, and for latent variables that are not normally distributed. Note, however, that a model defined as such is invariant under rotation of the latent variables and requires K additional identification restrictions (see Rijmen, 2009, for a detailed account). I therefore continue to assume independent (and normally distributed) latent variables in the remainder of this paper.

By including a specific dimension for each item block, the bifactor model accounts for the clustering effect of items within item blocks. However, in the PIRLS assessment, there is, as noted earlier, an additional level of nesting: items are nested within item blocks, which in turn are nested within purposes of reading. This additional level can be incorporated by adding an additional layer to the bifactor model. A model defined as such is again a hierarchical model, and could be called a trifactor model: every item depends on the overall reading literacy factor, a factor specific to the reading purpose that the item is assessing, and a specific factor for the item block to which the item belongs.

Figure 2 presents the directed acyclic graph for the trifactor model. The factors at the intermediate level of the hierarchy are denoted by θ_L (reading for literary experience) and θ_I (reading to acquire and use information). Using the graphical-modeling framework, one can show that maximum likelihood estimation of a trifactor model involves a sequence of computations in three-dimensional subspaces. Each subspace contains one latent variable for each of the three levels: an item block factor, a factor for the purpose of reading in which the item block is nested, and the overall factor.

Figure 2: Directed acyclic graph of a trifactor model

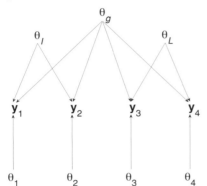

Higher-Order Models

Higher-order models offer an alternative approach for modeling a nested item structure. Like hierarchical models, higher-order models originate from factor analysis for continuous variables. However, analogous models can be formulated for discrete outcome variables.

The second-order multidimensional item response theory model that takes into account the effects of item blocks incorporates a specific dimension for each of them, just like the bifactor model. It also contains a general dimension. However, items do not directly depend on this general dimension as is the case in the bifactor model. Rather, items depend directly only on their respective specific dimensions, which, in turn, depend on the general dimension. It is assumed that the specific dimensions are conditionally independent; that is, the general dimension is assumed to take into account all associations among the specific dimensions. Figure 3 displays the directed acyclic graph for the second-order model.

The model equations for the second-order model defined for binary data are

$$g(\pi_j) = \alpha_{jk}\theta_k + \beta_j, \tag{3}$$

$$\theta_k = \alpha_{kg}\theta_g + \xi_k, \tag{4}$$

where α_{kg} indicates the extent to which the specific dimension θ_k is explained by the general dimension θ_g, and ξ_k is the part of θ_k that is unique. Because of the assumption that the general dimension accounts for all the dependencies between the specific dimensions, all ξ_k are assumed to be statistically independent from one another and from θ_g. Combining Equations 3 and 4 yields

$$g(\pi_j) = \alpha_{jk}\alpha_{kg}\theta_g + \alpha_{jk}\xi_k + \beta_j . \tag{5}$$

The second-order model is identified by assuming a standard normal distribution for the latent variables $(\theta_g, \xi_1 \dots, \xi_k)' \sim N(\mathbf{0}, \mathbf{I})$. A comparison of Equation 5 with Equation 2 shows that the second-order model is a restricted bifactor model, where, within each item block, the loadings on the specific dimensions are proportional to the

Figure 3: Directed acyclic graph of a second-order model

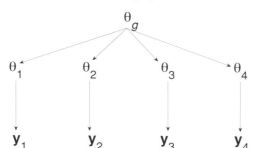

loadings on the general dimension. In general, a higher-order model can always be reformulated as a hierarchical model with proportionality constraints on the loadings (Yung, Thissen, & McLeod, 1999).

The second-order model for discrete observed variables was introduced in the literature on item response theory under the name of the testlet model (Bradlow, Wainer, & Wang, 1999; Wainer, Bradlow, & Wang, 2007). The fact that these authors used a slightly different notation may have contributed to the formal equivalence between the testlet model and a second-order model having generally been ignored.

Analogous to hierarchical models, higher-order models can be formulated for assessments in which items are nested at more than one level. In the context of the PIRLS assessment, a third-order model could be formulated. In this model, item blocks would constitute the first-order factors, purposes of reading the second-order factors, and reading literacy the single third-order factor. However, this third-order model is not identified without further constraints in the specific context of the PIRLS assessment because there are only two indicators for the overarching reading literacy factor (the two reading purposes). One way to identify the model is to impose an equality constraint on the loadings of the two reading-purpose factors on the third-order factor. Alternatively, a second-order model can be formulated with two correlated factors at the second level. I discuss this model in the next section.

Bifactor or Second-Order Model with a General Factor for Each Reading Purpose

Rather than specifying a third-order model for the PIRLS assessment, one can specify a second-order model with two correlated reading purpose factors at the second level (see Figure 4). Because of the undirected edge between θ_L and θ_I, the graph is no longer a directed graph but a chain graph. Analogously, a bifactor structure can be specified that incorporates two correlated dimensions instead of a single general dimension. Cai (2010) has proposed a similar model. Figure 5 presents a bifactor model with two correlated general dimensions.

Figure 4: Chain graph of a second-order model with a second-order factor for each reading purpose

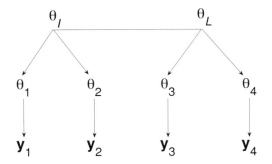

Figure 5: Chain graph of a bifactor model with a general factor for each reading purpose

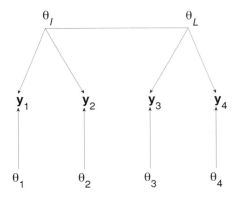

In principle, both models can be estimated with an efficient EM algorithm that involves computations in two-dimensional latent spaces. However, technically, when the latent variables are assumed to be normally distributed, the model is estimated through a Cholesky decomposition of the covariance matrix of the latent variables. As a consequence, one of the correlated reading purpose factors, say θ_L, is reformulated as a weighted sum of the other purpose factor, say θ_I, and an independent residual factor, say $\theta_{I, res}$. For the bifactor model, the items loading on θ_L are now loading on three dimensions: the item block factor θ_I and the residual purpose factor $\theta_{L, res}$. For the second-order factor, the item-block factors for the literacy item blocks now load on the uncorrelated factors θ_L and $\theta_{L, res}$. Therefore, computations in three-dimensional latent spaces are required in the expectation step of the efficient EM algorithm.

Double-Structure Bifactor Model

Although the models discussed up to now can be used to incorporate either the effects of item clustering within item blocks (and within purposes of reading) or the effects of items clustered within comprehension processes, they cannot take into account the crossed classification structure of item blocks with comprehension processes. Figure

6 presents a model that does take into account a crossed classification structure. The model contains a general factor and two sets of specific factors: one set for item blocks and another set for comprehension processes. To keep the visual representation clear, the figure represents only two comprehension processes: focus on and retrieve explicitly stated information (θ_F), and examine and evaluate content, language, and textual elements (θ_E). Note that because of the crossed classification structure, it is no longer possible to have a single node represent all of the items of a given item block. More specifically, this situation occurs because items within an item block relate to different comprehension processes.

Figure 6: Directed acyclic graph of a double-structure bifactor model

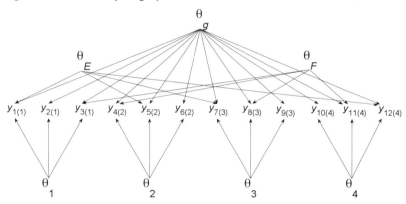

Similar model structures could be defined within a higher-order model structure. Furthermore, the additional nesting of item blocks within reading purposes could be incorporated by adding a layer for reading purposes on the item-block side of the model. In the context of factor analysis, the multitrait-multimethod model is also an example of a model with a crossed classification latent structure (Campbell & Fiske, 1959), which is most often defined for continuous outcome variables.

A feature that all double-structure models have in common is the fact that maximum likelihood estimation of such models scales with the smallest set of latent variables in them. Thus, for the model presented in Figure 6, maximum likelihood estimation would involve numerical integration over the sets of latent variables consisting of the general factor, one item block factor, and all of the four comprehension processes. This can be understood intuitively as follows: in the expectation step of the EM algorithm, the posterior probabilities of the latent variables, given the observed data, are computed. However, given that a response is observed, the latent variables for which the item is an indicator become conditionally dependent. For example, a person who gives a correct answer to a particular item is more likely to have a high level of reading literacy, *or* to be good at solving that particular item block, *or* to having mastered the involved comprehension process very well. Observing a high value on one of these three latent variables would make a high value on any of the other two latent variables less likely.

APPLICATION TO THE PIRLS 2006 ASSESSMENT

Description of the Dataset

The 2006 PIRLS assessment was administered in 40 countries, with a total student sample size of 215,137. The assessment contained five text passages for each reading purpose, with a total of 126 questions. The number of items within an item block varied from 11 to 14 items (Martin, Mullis, & Kennedy, 2007). A balanced incomplete booklet design was used, where each booklet consisted of two item blocks. Both constructed-response and multiple-choice items were included. All multiple-choice items were binary items, whereas some of the constructed-response items were partial credit items. In all analyses reported below, the logit link function was used for binary items, and the cumulative logit link function was used for polytomous items.

As is the case in other large-scale assessments, participants in PIRLS are sampled according to a complex two-stage clustered sampling design. The sampling design calls for the use of sampling weights during model estimation, as recently discussed by Rutkowski, Gonzalez, Joncas, and von Davier (2010). Within a country, sampling weights are computed as the inverse of the selection probability, and their sum approximates the size of the population (Foy & Kennedy, 2008). In situations in which data from several countries are combined, using these "total" weights would lead to results that are heavily influenced by the data from the large countries. Therefore, in the following analyses, "senate weights" were used. Senate weights are a renormalization of the total weights within each country so that they add up to the same constant for each country and thereby give equal weight to each country in the analyses.

Analysis Sequence

The modeling framework outlined in the previous sections is quite flexible. Consequently, the type and number of psychometric models that can be estimated from a given dataset become quite large. This calls for a strategy that allows one to determine which models to estimate. A sequential approach was followed in the present study. First, a unidimensional two-parameter logistic model was estimated. The unidimensional model served as the background model by which to evaluate the more complex models. Next, the effects of item blocks were taken into account through both a second-order and a bifactor model, with one general dimension and 10 specific dimensions (one for each testlet). Similarly, in order to take into account the effects of comprehension processes, both a second-order and a bifactor model were estimated, with one general dimension and a specific dimension for each of the four comprehension processes. Further models were specified contingent upon the results of these analyses, and therefore these models are not discussed until after presentation of the results for the bifactor and second-order models.

Results

The two-parameter logistic, the bifactor, and the second-order models

The top six rows of Table 1 present the number of parameters, the number of dimensions, the deviance, and the Akaike information criterion (AIC) (Akaike, 1973) for the two-parameter logistic, the bifactor, and the second-order models. The two-parameter model was estimated with both 10 and 20 quadrature points, whereas 10 quadrature points were used for all multidimensional models. The individual contributions of the tested students to the log-likelihood were weighted by their sampling weights.

Table 1: The number of parameters, number of dimensions, deviance, and Akaike information criterion (AIC) for the estimated models

	#Par	#Dim	Deviance	AIC
2PL_10	290	1	706956	707386
2PL_20	290	1	706431	707011
BF_IB	415	11	704925	**705755**
2O_IB	300	11	705603	706203
BF_CP	415	5	705965	706795
2O_CP	294	5	706743	707331
2D2PL	291	2	706161	706743
2DBF_IB	416	12	704757	**705569**

Note: #Par = number of parameters; #Dim = number of dimensions; AIC = Akaike information criterion; 2PL_10 = two-parameter logistic model with 10 quadrature points; 2PL_20 = two-parameter logistic model with 20 quadrature points; BF_IB = bifactor model with item blocks as specific dimensions; 2O_IB = second-order model with item blocks as specific dimensions; BF_CP = bifactor model with comprehension processes as specific dimensions; 2O_CP = second-order model with comprehension processes as specific dimensions; 2D2PL = between-item two-dimensional two-parameter logistic model with reading purposes as dimensions; 2DBF_IB = bifactor model with item blocks as specific dimensions and two, general dimensions representing reading purposes.

According to the AIC, the bifactor model with specific factors corresponding to item blocks emerged as the preferred model. Closer inspection of the item-parameter estimates reveals whether this model provided a better fit to the data. In Figures 7a–j, the loadings of the items on the specific dimensions are plotted against the item loadings on the general dimension, separately for each item block. Although the loadings on the specific dimensions are smaller than the loadings on the general dimension, many of them are still substantially different from zero. This pattern explains why the bifactor model provides a better fit than the two-parameter logistic model. The results vary somewhat across item blocks. For the item block labeled "Antarctica" (Figure 7f), all loadings on the specific dimensions are close to zero, except for one item that has an outlying estimated value of 3.04. For four item blocks (see Figures 7c, 7f, 7i, and 7j), the loadings on the specific dimensions are negative for some items and positive for other items, indicating both negative and positive conditional dependencies, given the general dimension. For the six other item blocks, all loadings on the specific dimension are larger than zero, indicating that all conditional dependencies are positive for the items in those item blocks.

It is furthermore clear from Figures 7a–j that, for most item blocks, the loadings on the specific dimension are not proportional to the loadings on the general dimension. If this were the case, the dots within each figure would form approximately a straight line. The lack of proportionality within each item block is a violation of the assumption of the second-order model, since the second-order model is a bifactor model in which the loadings on the specific dimension are constrained to be proportional to the loadings on the general dimension within each item block. The lack of proportionality of the loadings explains why the bifactor model provides a better fit to the data then the second-order model.

For the bifactor model in which the comprehension processes constituted the specific dimensions, the loadings on the specific dimensions were closer to zero than was the case for the bifactor model with item blocks as specific dimensions. These means were heavily influenced by some outlying estimated values for the bifactor model with comprehension processes as specific dimensions. The median value of the loadings on the specific dimensions amounted to 0.15 for this model, which is less than half of the median for the bifactor model with item blocks as specific dimensions (0.32). These results may explain why the bifactor model with the item blocks as specific dimensions provided a better fit than the bifactor model with the comprehension processes as specific dimensions.

Figure 7 a–j: Scatter plots of the loadings on the general dimension versus the loadings on the specific dimensions for the bifactor model with item blocks as specific dimensions

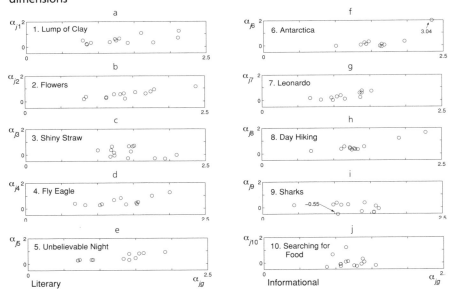

Note: For the "Antarctica" item block, one loading on the specific dimensions was truncated at 2.0 in Panel 6. For the "Sharks" item block, one loading on the specific dimensions was truncated at -0.5 in Panel 9.

In terms of model fit, it pays to incorporate item-cluster effects that stem from the item blocks rather than to incorporate item-cluster effects related to comprehension processes. Another indication that taking into account the comprehension processes does not have a substantial impact is that the deviance for the second-order model with comprehension processes as first-order dimensions has a higher deviance than the unidimensional two-parameter logistic model with 20 quadrature points. It seems that increasing the quadrature points from 10 to 20 for the two-parameter logistic model leads to more model-fit improvement than does modeling the comprehension processes with a second-order model.

From the first set of estimated models, it is apparent that the item blocks do constitute a separate source of individual differences. In contrast, the four comprehension processes do not seem to constitute separate dimensions, but rather are blended together into one overall dimension.

Models incorporating dimensions for purposes of reading
Because item blocks are nested within two purposes of reading, a valid question is whether the effects of item blocks that were found in the previous section are effects that can be attributed to the item blocks per se, or whether these effects merely reflect individual differences linked to the two different purposes of reading. In order to investigate this matter further, two more models were estimated: a between-item two-dimensional model, with one dimension corresponding to each reading purpose, and a bifactor model with specific dimensions corresponding to item blocks and with two general dimensions, one for each reading purpose (see Figure 5). The corresponding higher-order models were not considered because the results presented in the previous section indicated that the second-order model structure was less suited to the PIRLS 2006 dataset. The last two lines of Table 1 present the number of parameters, number of dimensions, deviance, and AIC for these two models.

The two-dimensional two-parameter logistic model provided a better fit than the unidimensional two-parameter logistic model, but it was not as good as the bifactor model with item blocks as specific dimensions. The estimated correlation between the two purposes of reading was 0.91. A visual inspection of the scatterplot revealed that the estimated loadings were very similar for the two-dimensional and unidimensional two-parameter logistic models.

After the item blocks had been taken into account through the incorporation of specific dimensions corresponding to item blocks, it was evident that the model with a separate dimension for each of the two reading purposes provided a better fit than the corresponding model with only a single general dimension, according to the AIC. The correlation between the two reading purposes was 0.93. A visual inspection of the scatterplots revealed that the estimated loadings were very similar to the bifactor model with one general dimension. This was the case for both the general dimensions and the specific dimensions corresponding to item blocks. The median of the loadings on the specific dimensions was 0.23, which is about one third lower than the median of the loadings on the specific dimensions for the bifactor model with a single general dimension.

Overall, the results indicate that the effect of item blocks can be attributed in part but not entirely to the fact that item blocks are clustered within reading purposes. However, the high correlations between the two reading purposes in the two models presented in this section, and the fact that the item loadings were very similar between the models with one general dimension and the models with a dimension for each reading purpose, indicate that the two purposes of reading do not constitute substantially different sources of individual differences; rather, they blend together into one overall dimension for reading.

CONCLUDING REMARKS

The items of large-scale assessments are often clustered at multiple levels. For example, the items used in PIRLS are clustered within item blocks related to text materials, which are further clustered within two purposes of reading. At the same time, items can be clustered according to comprehension processes. The clustering according to comprehension processes is crossed with the clustering within item blocks and reading purposes.

Several multidimensional item response theory models were presented. The models differ with respect to *how* clustering effects were taken into account; that is, they incorporated a hierarchical versus a higher-order structure. The presented models also differ with respect to the *degree* to which clustering effects were taken into account.

Some of the models presented have been previously proposed as multidimensional item response theory models. In particular, Gibbons and Hedeker (1992) presented the bifactor model for categorical data, while Bradlow and colleagues presented a second-order model (see Bradlow et al., 1999; Wainer et al., 2007). Although the more complex models presented in this paper have not been examined in the context of item response theory models, related models have been proposed in the context of factor analysis. But what is of more importance than the degree to which the proposed models are new is the explicit recognition that all of these models can be embedded within a graphical model framework for latent variable models (Rijmen, 2008, 2010, in press).

Through the application of algorithms operating on the graphical representation of the models, the conditional independence relations implied by the structure of the model can be exploited, leading to efficient maximum likelihood estimation methods. What determines the computational burden of a model is not so much its dimensionality as whether or not the latent variables of the model can be partitioned into conditionally independent subsets, after observation of the data. It is crucial to realize that prior independence of latent variables does not imply that they are independent after observation of the responses. For example, all latent variables of the model that incorporates latent variables for both item blocks and comprehension processes (the double structure model depicted in Figure 6) are assumed to be independent a priori. However, given the observed item responses, a complex dependency structure arises, as I explained when discussing the double structure model.

A sequence of models was fitted to the complete PIRLS 2006 dataset. The results indicated substantial item clustering effects related to the organization of items within item blocks. In contrast, the effects of comprehension processes and purposes of reading were minor. The loadings of the items on the specific dimensions corresponding to comprehension processes were quite low, and the correlation between the two dimensions corresponding to the two purposes of reading was very high. The loadings on the specific dimensions corresponding to item blocks remained substantial after taking into account the clustering of items within the two purposes of reading. Taken together, the findings suggest that design factors such as item blocks are more substantial sources of residual dependencies between items than content factors such as comprehension processes and purposes of reading.

References

Akaike, H. (1973). Information theory and an extension of the maximum likelihood principle. In B. N. Petrov & F. Csáki (Eds.), *Proceedings of the Second International Symposium on Information Theory* (pp. 267–281). Budapest, Hungary: Akadémiai Kaidó.

Bradlow, E. T., Wainer, H., & Wang, X. (1999). A Bayesian random effects model for testlets. *Psychometrika*, *64*, 153–168.

Cai, L. (2010). A two-tier full-information item factor analysis model with applications. *Psychometrika*, *75*, 581–612 .

Campbell, D. T., & Fiske, D. W. (1959). Convergent and discriminant validation by the multitrait-multimethod matrix. *Psychological Bulletin*, *56*, 81–105.

Fahrmeir, L., & Tutz, G. (2001). *Multivariate statistical modelling based on generalized linear models* (2nd ed.). New York, NY: Springer.

Foy, P., & Kennedy, A. M. (2008). *PIRLS 2006 user guide for the international database*. Chestnut Hill, MA: TIMSS & PIRLS International Study Center, Boston College.

Gibbons, R. D., & Hedeker, D. (1992). Full-information item bi-factor analysis. *Psychometrika*, *57*, 423–436.

Holzinger, K. J., & Swineford, F. (1937). The bi-factor method. *Psychometrika*, *2*, 41–54.

Martin, M. O., Mullis, I. V. S., & Kennedy, A. M. (2007). *PIRLS 2006 technical report*. Chestnut Hill, MA: TIMSS & PIRLS International Study Center, Boston College.

Mullis, I. V. S., Kennedy, A. M., Martin, M. O., & Sainsbury, M. (2006). *PIRLS 2006 assessment framework and specifications* (2nd ed.). Chestnut Hill, MA: TIMSS & PIRLS International Study Center, Boston College.

Rijmen, F. (2009). *An efficient EM algorithm for multidimensional IRT models: Full information maximum likelihood estimation in limited time* (ETS Research Report RR-09-03). Princeton, NJ: ETS.

Rijmen, F. (2010). Formal relations and an empirical comparison between the bi-factor, the testlet, and a second-order multidimensional IRT model. *Journal of Educational Measurement*, *47*, 361–372.

Rijmen, F. (in press). The use of graphs in latent variable modeling: Beyond visualization. In G. R. Hancock (Ed.), Advances in latent class analysis: *A festschrift in honor of C. Mitchell Dayton*. Charlotte, NC: Information Age Publishing.

Rijmen, F., Vansteelandt, K., & De Boeck, P. (2008). Latent class models for diary method data: Parameter estimation by local computations. *Psychometrika*, *73*, 167–182.

Rutkowski, L., Gonzalez, E., Joncas, M., & von Davier, M. (2010). International large-scale assessment data: Issues in secondary analysis and reporting. *Educational Researcher*, *39*, 142–151.

TIMSS & PIRLS International Study Center, Boston College. (2010). *About PIRLS*. Retrieved from http://timss.bc.edu/pirls2006/about.html

Wainer, H., Bradlow, E. T., & Wang, X. (2007). *Testlet response theory and its applications*. New York, NY: Cambridge University Press.

Yung, Y.-F., Thissen, D., & McLeod, L. D. (1999). On the relationship between the higher-order factor model and the hierarchical factor model. *Psychometrika*, *64*, 113–128.

Diagnostic cluster analysis of mathematics skills

Yoon Soo Park and Young-Sun Lee
Teachers College, Columbia University, New York, USA

Clustering and similarity trees are effective techniques for grouping and visualizing related objects; they can be implemented to assess how individuals think of psychological concepts. This study examined a method of clustering attributes required to solve mathematics problems by mapping item responses to an attribute matrix and from there conducting *K*-means clustering and hierarchical agglomerative cluster analysis (HACA). The analysis was broadened to examine how the extended similarity tree (EXTREE) algorithm (Corter & Tversky, 1986) can be used to illustrate the hierarchical and overlapping nature of the fine-grained attributes required to solve mathematics test items. Twenty-five items from the TIMSS 2007 Grade 4 mathematics test were used to generate a list of skills or attributes that together constituted a Q-matrix (Embretson, 1984; Tatsuoka, 1985). High-performing countries (Hong Kong SAR and Chinese Taipei), average-performing countries (Denmark, Sweden, and the United States), and low-performing countries (Colombia, Kuwait, Qatar, and Yemen) were selected to examine attribute-structure differences across countries, while two high-performing benchmark participants—the states of Massachusetts and Minnesota in the United States—were selected to examine attribute-structure differences within a country. Results showed that the structure of attributes in the higher-performing countries had a clearer, more hierarchical structure than the structure of attributes evident in the lower-performing countries. Examining cluster structures of attributes can thus serve as a useful method for exploring the structure of attributes and providing diagnostic feedback to policymakers and educational researchers on areas where students may need further instruction.

IERI Monograph Series: Issues and Methodologies in Large-Scale Assessments Volume 4

INTRODUCTION

Scholars and policymakers have for a long time used broad domain-based scores from international assessments to modify and attempt to improve their countries' education systems. Using these indicators, researchers have examined measures governing the curricula and textbooks used in their countries (Hook, Bishop, & Hook, 2007; McNeely, 1997) as well as the quality of their teachers and teacher education (Rautalin & Alasuutari, 2007; Simola, 2005). Researchers have also used these indicators to conduct cross-national explorations of teaching practices and patterns of teaching (Givvin, Hiebert, Jacobs, Hollingsworth, & Gallimore, 2005; Hiebert et al., 2005), instructional methods (House, 2005), curricula and education systems (Menon, 2000), and attitudinal or instructional components (Papanastasiou, 2002). There has, however, been relatively little cross-national comparative research into how students in different countries or regions within countries respond to curricular materials.

More specifically, the outcomes of analyses designed to explore the relationship between the specific skills (or, to use a broader term, attributes) that students need to solve a particular test item and how that relationship can be confounded by other related skills provide important understandings for instructors. Often, students answer a mathematics test item incorrectly not only because of their arithmetic miscalculation, but also because they confuse the skill they need to apply to a specific learning area with the skill or skills they need for another learning area (Cai, 2007; Kuhs & Ball, 1986; Lubienski, 2000). For students, the ability to identify whether they need to apply a specific skill or set of skills with respect to a specific learning area, or whether they think they can apply the same skills or sets of skills to two or more learning areas, can serve as an important learning aid.

The Trends in Mathematics and Science Study (TIMSS) provides an opportunity to explore not only how students within a country and across countries perceive the utility of certain skills relative to a learning area, but also whether those skills link with other skills. TIMSS, which has been conducted since 1995 and had 43 participating countries in the 2007 administration at Grade 4, provides data that allows each participating country to determine the relative standing of its students' mathematics performance within an international context. The released data also offer information that policymakers and educators can use when developing measures designed to improve their education systems (Cai & Silver, 1995).

To date, most researchers have relied solely on using the overall mean proficiency scores of each country or the overall scores of students on the content and cognitive domains assessed by TIMSS to analyze the performance of the students within their own country or relative to the other participating countries. Despite the complexity and the richness of the data collected, TIMSS has been criticized for lacking studies that can be directed toward improving student performance at the attribute level. As a response to this criticism, this study extends beyond merely using overall proficiency scores to analyze student performance. Instead, we use students' response patterns on TIMSS test items to gain an understanding of which attributes, whether single or in association with others, students seem to see as necessary to solve the problem embedded within a specific item.

The skills that TIMSS assesses relate to three main content domains: number, geometric shapes and measurement, and data and display. Each domain, in turn, contains several "fine-grained" topic areas. The number domain covers, for example, whole numbers, fractions, and decimals, number sentences with whole numbers, and patterns and relationships. The geometric shapes and measurement domain focuses on lines and angles, two- and three-dimensional shapes, and location and movement. The data and display domain includes reading and interpreting, and organizing and representing. These topic areas were developed from the TIMSS framework (Mullis, Martin, Ruddock, O'Sullivan, Arora, & Erberber, 2005), such that the content areas associated with an item can be mapped onto the specific skills or attributes students need to apply when solving a particular problem.

The analytic framework of TIMSS yields an ideal platform from which to conduct multivariate methods of cluster analysis. These methods generate visualizations useful for exploring similarities and dissimilarities in data. Clustering and similarity trees are particularly effective techniques for grouping related objects, and their use can help researchers determine how individuals think with respect to psychological concepts. Because multiple attributes are required to solve a particular item, investigating how students perceive these specific attributes—whether they view them as distinct objects or cluster them with other attributes—can provide additional information useful for instructors. If subsets of attributes emerge as being grouped together, the next step is to identify which are held in common and to investigate why they are related. Additionally, if their grouping is hierarchical in nature, determining the likely reason for such a structure should also prove useful.

Attributes can be grouped into clusters using the K-means method (MacQueen, 1967) or formulated to explore their hierarchical nature via the hierarchical agglomerative cluster analysis (HACA; Hartigan, 1975). They can also be analyzed through use of the extended similarity tree method (Corter & Tversky, 1986). This last approach, which is also known as EXTREE, allows simultaneous examination of attributes' hierarchical and overlapping features. However, in order to incorporate attributes into the response data, the aforementioned methods of cluster analysis, unlike traditional methods of cluster analysis, require the attributes to be specified in an incidence matrix, that is, a Q-matrix (Embretson, 1984; Tatsuoka, 1985). This matrix maps the fine-grained attributes that a test-taker needs to solve a particular item correctly. Associations between the attributes can then be transformed into measures of distance and, from there, examined via the clustering and similarity trees analyses, with respect to group-related attributes and with respect to how students from a particular country utilize these attributes when problem-solving.

In this study, we analyzed 25 items from the TIMSS 2007 Grade 4 mathematics assessment in order to examine the clustering of attributes required to solve these items. We then used the K-means, HACA, and EXTREE methods to examine the clusters. We framed the results from the cluster analyses to answer these three questions:

1. What types of attribute clusters emerge during examination of how Grade 4 students solve mathematics problems?

2. How do these clusters of attributes differ among high-, average-, and low-performing countries and regions within the same country?

3. What are the differences and similarities with respect to how students studying within different education systems, under different curriculum configurations, and from different textbooks perceive and process the fine-grained attributes needed to answer mathematics test items?

For the comparative purposes of the study, we used the overall average test scale score for each of the participating TIMSS 2007 countries to select nine countries. These were Hong Kong SAR (henceforth, Hong Kong), which was ranked first on the international achievement scale, Chinese Taipei (Taiwan), which ranked third, the United States (13th), Denmark (15th), Sweden (24th), Colombia (37th), Kuwait (41st), Qatar (42nd), and Yemen (43rd). The first two countries represent countries where student performance was, on average, high. The next three countries represent average performance, and the final four, low performance. We then examined how the students in these countries perceived and processed the attributes prescribed in the Q-matrix. In order to compare how these clusters differed within the United States, we also drew on data from two American states that elected to participate in TIMSS 2007 as benchmarking participants.[1] The two states were Massachusetts, which ranked fourth on the international achievement scale, and Minnesota, which ranked sixth. They followed the same procedure to administer the TIMSS test to their students that the 43 countries used.[2]

CLUSTER ANALYSIS FOR COGNITIVE DIAGNOSIS

Cluster analysis models are based on measures of proximity, such as similarities or dissimilarities, which represent the degree of correspondence among objects across all others used in the analysis (Hair, Black, Babin, Anderson, & Tatham, 2006). Previous studies have examined clustering of items. Beller (1990), for example, used a multidimensional scaling (MDS) model (smallest space analysis) and a hierarchical clustering method (additive tree model) to study the interrelationships among items. The two methods differ in that the former represents objects in a continuous multidimensional space, whereas the latter classifies objects into discrete clusters (Shepard, 1980; Shepard & Arabie, 1979).

---

1 Regions or countries that elect to participate in TIMSS as benchmarking participants do so because they want "to assess the comparative international standing of their students' achievement and to view their curriculum and instruction in an international context" (IES National Center for Education Statistics, n.d., state/district participation section).

2 In the rest of this paper, we use the term "regions" when referring to both the countries and the two states.

Beller's (1990) study showed that the hierarchical clustering method demonstrated more interpretable and meaningful results than the MDS with respect to identifying the structure of tests and their items. Sireci and Geisinger (1992) used a combination of MDS analysis and hierarchical clustering analysis to evaluate the content representation of a test. They found that this approach was effective in showing the correspondence between item similarity ratings from judges and the item groupings prescribed in the test blueprint. Corter (1995) examined clusters using subtraction-fraction items to verify the attributes required to solve the items. He used cluster methods that included the EXTREE (Corter & Tversky, 1986) approach for investigating hierarchical and overlapping features in order to calculate and analyze measures of similarity. The results of this study confirmed EXTREE as a useful tool for validating matrices of attribute specification.

Other researchers have examined other methods of clustering examinees. These methods require the specification of a matrix that indicates the attributes required for solving an item (i.e., Q-matrix). Using this matrix and the item responses of examinees, Chiu, Douglas, and Li (2009) conducted a cluster analysis designed to group individuals who possessed the same skills. Chiu et al. (2009) showed that this technique was nearly as effective a method as latent class models for the purposes of cognitive diagnosis. Chiu and Seo (2009) applied this method to the 2001 Progress in International Reading and Literacy Study (PIRLS) in order to demonstrate its implementation in practice.

Another type of clustering methodology is the rule space methodology or RSM (Tatsuoka, 1985), which has been used to classify students into a dichotomous pattern of attribute mastery and non-mastery (i.e., knowledge states). The RSM uses the Q-matrix to generate a probability that a given student belongs to a probable knowledge state, based on his or her response patterns. Gierl (2007) proposed a version of the RSM pertaining to the attribute hierarchy method (AHM), which is based on the hierarchies of skills evident in a performance task.

Applications of RSM have been widely studied, including within the context of analyses of data from international comparative assessments such as TIMSS. Dogan and Tatsuoka (2008) used the RSM to analyze the mastery levels of Turkish students and of American students who participated in TIMSS 1999. They found that the Turkish students had weaker algebra and probability/statistics skills than the American students. Um, Dogan, Im, Tatsuoka, and Corter (2003) conducted a similar study. They compared student attribute mastery in Korea, the Czech Republic, and the United States. Using data from 20 countries that participated in the TIMSS 1999-Repeat assessment, Tatsuoka, Corter, and Tatsuoka (2004) examined students' mastery of 23 attributes by comparing their mean mastery levels. They found a high association between mastery of TIMSS geometry items and mathematical thinking skills—skills that were lacking among the United States students.

Birenbaum, Tatsuoka, and Yamada (2004) also used the TIMSS 1999-Repeat data to compare the attribute mastery of students in the United States, Japan, and Israel.

This study additionally examined the performance of Jewish and Arab students in Israel who were studying the same curriculum. Results showed that Japanese students outperformed the students in the other two countries and that the attribute patterns of the Jewish students were significantly more effective than the attribute patterns of the Arab students in terms of correct answers on the TIMSS items. Chen, Gorin, Thompson, and Tatsuoka (2008) studied the performance data of culturally diverse groups on the TIMSS 1999-Repeat assessment. They compared the Taiwanese and American students and used the fit of the RSM as a measure to validate the equivalence of the achievement scale scores of these two student cohorts. Based on the results of classification rates and the prediction of scores, they concluded that a cognitive-psychometric modeling approach such as the RSM is useful for exploring issues related to score validity.

In summary, various researchers have examined clustering of items and examinees in an effort to identify the cognitive diagnostic properties of large-scale achievement tests and the performance of students in relation to those attributes. There have also been many applications of RSM using the TIMSS data. However, in both cases, only a few studies exist in which the researchers involved specifically investigated the clustering of attributes.

The Sum-Score Matrix

As described in Chiu et al. (2009), cluster analysis models used to diagnose cognitive performance require a measure of examinee scores for each attribute. However, this measure needs to be created through the use of two matrices: one that consists of the item responses (correct or incorrect) of test-takers, and one that maps the relationships between the items and attributes required to solve the item (i.e., Q-matrix). Therefore, the primary consideration resides in constructing the Q-matrix (Embretson, 1984; Tatsuoka, 1985), while the secondary consideration focuses on combining the two matrices. The two matrices are combined in order to create a matrix that represents a sum score of a particular attribute; this matrix thus represents both examinee response patterns as well as the attribute specification for each item. Finally, the ensuing matrix should be transformed into a measure of distance that is subsequently used to conduct the cluster analysis.

In the remainder of this section of our paper, we discuss the theory underpinning the following steps: (a) combining the response data to the Q-matrix using the sum-score matrix, (b) transforming the combined matrix into a measure of distance (here we also explain the different measures and their implications), and (c) conducting the K-means analysis, the HACA, and the extended similarity tree (EXTREE) analysis. As we noted earlier, the K-means and the HACA are methods commonly used to group and examine the hierarchical structure of the clusters, respectively, whereas the EXTREE method handles both overlapping and hierarchical features of the clusters simultaneously, which is an advantage of its use.

A Q-matrix can be constructed by defining q_{jk} to be an incidence matrix, with value "1" signaling the requirement of the attribute and "0" representing otherwise for item $j=\{1,2,...,J\}$ and attribute $k=\{1,2,...,K\}$. Therefore, this framework allows the formation of a J x K binary matrix; the element in the jth row and kth column of the matrix, q_{jk}, corresponds to whether the kth attribute is required to solve the jth item correctly. Validating the Q-matrix requires multiple coders to independently assign binary values to the matrix and to generate a finalized Q-matrix through discussion and consensus. However, depending on the type of problem embedded in a test item, the Q-matrix can vary by coder, because test-takers can use different approaches to solve an item. However, when specifying the final Q-matrix used for a study, researchers should use the most dominant method, as validated by domain experts.

The finalized Q-matrix is combined with the item responses of the test-takers to generate examinee scores for each attribute, which are then used in the subsequent cluster analysis. If we let Y_{ij} be examinee i's response for item j, such that $i=\{1,2,...,I\}$ and $j=\{1,2,...,J\}$, then this step becomes tantamount to combining the I x J matrix with the J x K matrix. Although various formulations can be used to join the two matrices, we used the sum-scores matrix that Chiu et al. (2009) employed. Thus:

$$W_{ik} = \sum_{j=1}^{J} Y_{ij} \; q_{jk}.$$

Here, the vector $\underline{W}_i = (W_{i1}, W_{i2},... W_{iK})'$ is the score profile of the attributes for examinee i that is derived from their item responses in Y_{ij}. In other words, the vector is similar to a score for each attribute for examinee i, weighted by the number of times attribute k was required across items. By using the matrix W_{ik}, researchers can create a similarity or dissimilarity matrix that represents the distances between the attributes and which can then be used to conduct the cluster analysis.

Measures of Similarity and Dissimilarity

Although measures of correlation can be used to associate multivariate measures, distance measures are most commonly applied. These represent similarity as the proximity of observations to one another across variables in the cluster. In fact, distance measures are measures of dissimilarity, because larger distance measures represent less similarity. Therefore, to create measures of similarity, an inverse relationship is often used. A proximity distance, which represents the nearness of two objects, r and s, must satisfy the following three conditions:

1. $d_{(\underline{w}_i, \underline{w}_{i'})} \geq 0$ for all $\underline{w}_i$ and $\underline{w}_{i'}$,
2. $d_{(\underline{w}_i, \underline{w}_{i'})} = 0$ if, and only if, $\underline{w}_i = \underline{w}_{i'}$, and
3. $d_{(\underline{w}_i, \underline{w}_{i'})} = d_{(\underline{w}_{i'}, \underline{w}_i)}$.

Various measures that satisfy these conditions have been developed. These include the Euclidean distance, the squared Euclidean distance, the city-block distance, the Chebychev distance, and the Mahalanobis distance. A general metric used for distances is the Minkowski p-metric (Hair et al., 2006), which can be generalized to other forms of distances by varying p. For two K-dimensional datapoints $\underline{w}_i$ and $\underline{w}_{i'}$, the following equation defines the Minkowski distance:

$$d_{L_p}(\underline{w}_i, \underline{w}_{i'}) = [\sum_{k=1}^{K}(|w_{ik} - w_{i'k}|)^p]^{\frac{1}{p}}.$$

This equation requires the triangle inequality $d_{(\underline{w}_i, \underline{w}_{i'})} \leq d_{(\underline{w}_i, \underline{w}_{i''})} + d_{(\underline{w}_{i''}, \underline{w}_{i'})}$ to be satisfied. The Minkowski metric can be simplified to form the Euclidean distance when $p = 2$. The Mahalonabis distance is another popular distance measure. It takes into account the covariance between the variables $d_M(\underline{w}_i, \underline{w}_{i'}) = (\underline{w}_i - \underline{w}_{i'})^T \Sigma^{-1}(\underline{w}_i - \underline{w}_{i'})$, where Σ is the covariance matrix of W_{ik}, which is inversed and used as a weight.

Figure 1 shows a representation of a distance measure between two objects for variables X and Y using Euclidean distances. We have provided a simplified illustration of the Euclidean distance given that this distance measure can be generalized to other forms of distances. Figure 1 thus demonstrates how distance measures are *generally* calculated.

Figure 1: An example of Euclidean distance between two objects on variables X and Y

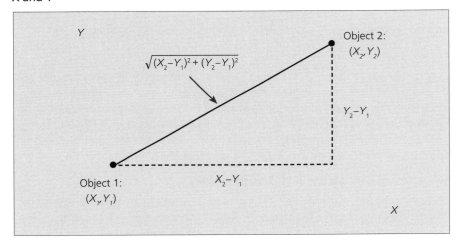

K-means, HACA, and Extended Similarity Tree

The key task with respect to the *K*-means algorithm is that of estimating the cluster centers based on the data, with the number of clusters being predetermined. In *K*-means clustering, the object $\underline{w}_i$ is assigned to cluster m, using, for example, the Euclidean distance:

$$m = \arg \min_{u \in \{1,2...,M\}} ||\underline{w}_i - \hat{\underline{c}}_u||^2 .$$

Here, $\hat{\underline{c}}_u$ is the estimated center of the uth cluster derived from the average of the observations within the cluster. The use of M initial K-dimensional clusters requires datapoints to be assigned to clusters by way of the above constraint. The cluster centers are then reset by calculating the average of assigned observations. This process is looped until relocation of observations is exhausted.

While the K-means algorithm groups clusters to exclusive clusters, the HACA involves a quite different approach. The hierarchical structure of the data is explored by taking into account distances between clusters in addition to distances between the data. Computationally, HACA is much simpler than the K-means. Again using the Euclidean distance as an example, we can define the initial distance matrix for two objects as $d_{ii'} = \sqrt{\sum_{k=1}^{K}(|w_{ik} - w_{i'k}|)^2}$. Each object thus initially begins with its own cluster. Having defined the distance between two clusters C_l and $C_{l'}$ as $d^*_{ll'}$, our next step is to cluster the two objects i and i' according to which $d^*_{ll'} = d_{ll'}$ is the smallest. For each additional step, two clusters are grouped to achieve the minimum distance by adjoining two of the existing clusters. From here on, the cluster distances are modified after each new join, and the algorithm will vary according to the linkage chosen. This iterative process is continued until all clusters are exhausted. (For further details, refer to Chiu et al., 2009.)

The extended similarity tree (EXTREE) algorithm can be divided into a three-step process (Corter & Tversky, 1986):

1. Obtaining a best-fit additive tree;

2. Estimating a measure of each possible marked feature and selecting the optimal set; and

3. Using a least-squares method to simultaneously estimate all model parameters.

The first step transforms data to satisfy the metric axioms. The neighbor score matrix is then calculated and joined to elements that are mutual nearest-neighbors (MNN), a process that satisfies the following equation:

If $c_{ij} = \max(c_{ik}, \forall k \neq i)$ and $c_{ji} = \max(c_{jk}, \forall k \neq i)$, then i, j is MNN.

This process is looped until all possible combinations are exhausted. The next process eliminates measure of the possible marked feature and picks the best group via the following equation:

$$W_A = \frac{1}{2N} \sum_Q [d(x, v) = d(y,u) - d(x,u) - d(y,u)].$$

This step allows both the elimination of redundant features and clique selection of pair-wise features. Finally, the least-squares method is used to estimate the parameters.

The advantage of using the EXTREE model over hierarchical or addtree models is that it allows the graphical representation of overlapping or non-nested features. It also allows the illustration of both common features as well as unique features. These strengths make the EXTREE model ideal for our study because it investigates attributes used to solve mathematics problems and that tend to have overlapping features.

In contrast to models for cognitive diagnosis, which classify test respondents (see, for example, Rupp & Templin, 2008; Tatsuoka, 1983; von Davier, 2005), the methods that we present in this study cluster attributes. We used all three of the above methods for this process. We based our definition of proximity across attributes on distance measures, which allowed us to examine, using the vector of student responses as a basis, which attributes were more similar and which were more distinct in terms of their relative distance.

METHOD

Data

Forty-three countries participated in the TIMSS 2007 Grade 4 mathematics assessment, which generated data from over 360,000 students (Olson, Martin, & Mullis, 2009). Raw data for the analyses were obtained from Boston College's TIMSS website and were converted to SAS data files via use of a modified SAS macro provided by the website; the file was scored and merged according to guidelines supplied by Foy and Olson (2009).

The TIMSS released dataset contains selected items and groups of examinees. We selected data from Blocks 4 and 5 for analysis because they encompass the greatest number of dichotomous items (23 dichotomous items out of 25 total items), a situation that eliminated the need to consider scores with partial credit. Out of the total 25 items used for this study, only two items (Items 12 and 21) were originally scored polytomously, with a maximum score of 2, rather than 1. We dichotomized these polytomous responses by treating responses with partial credit as incorrect and responses with full credit as correct. We also scored as incorrect omitted or unreached items.

As we stated above, we selected for the purposes of our study 11 regions based on their overall TIMSS ranking. Table 1 shows the rank, sample size, and the mean proficiency scores for these nine countries as well as for the two American states that took part in TIMSS as benchmarking participants.

Table 1: Mean proficiency statistics for the TIMSS 2007 Grade 4 participants

Performance	Rank	Country	Sample size	Mean proficiency	Standard error
High	1	Hong Kong SAR	3,791	606.80	3.58
	3	Chinese Taipei	4,131	575.82	1.73
	4	Massachusetts, USA*	1,747	572.48	3.51
	6	Minnesota, USA*	1,846	554.12	5.86
Average	13	United States	7,896	529.01	2.45
	15	Denmark	3,519	523.11	2.40
	24	Sweden	4,676	502.57	2.53
Low	37	Colombia	4,801	355.45	4.97
	41	Kuwait	3,803	315.54	3.65
	42	Qatar	7,019	296.27	1.04
	43	Yemen	5,811	223.68	5.97

Notes:
Based on TIMSS 2007 technical report (Olson et al., 2009).
* Regional entities.

Development of the Q-matrix

As described earlier in this paper, a Q-matrix is a table of skills that indicates whether an attribute is required for an item. When conducting our study, we used the TIMSS framework (Mullis et al., 2005) to identify 15 attributes derived from the 25 items. The TIMSS framework identifies 38 objectives. Using as our reference the list of attributes required to correctly solve an item, we modified and simplified the framework to complement the 25 items so that it represented two blocks of the TIMSS 2007 Grade 4 mathematics assessment. Figure 2 demonstrates how we created the Q-matrix for one of the items that we used in this study. Table 2 presents the list of attributes that we used to develop the Q-matrix. The table also presents the number of times each attribute was specified.

Although we combined and/or modified some objectives, the topic areas were preserved to an extent that enabled us to create 15 attributes that were not only fine-grained enough to allow us to make meaningful statements about the specific skills, but also small enough to prevent the measurement errors for each attribute from becoming too large. The average number of attributes required by all 25 items was 2.80. Three items required a single attribute, eight required two attributes, another eight required three attributes, and four required four attributes. The remaining two items required five and six attributes respectively.

Figure 2: Illustration of the *Q*-matrix specification for TIMSS Item 14

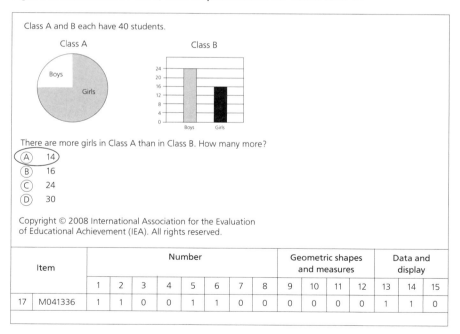

Class A and B each have 40 students.

Class A Class B

There are more girls in Class A than in Class B. How many more?

(A) 14
(B) 16
(C) 24
(D) 30

Item		Number								Geometric shapes and measures				Data and display		
		1	2	3	4	5	6	7	8	9	10	11	12	13	14	15
17	M041336	1	1	0	0	1	1	0	0	0	0	0	0	1	1	0

Table 2: Attributes developed from the 2007 TIMSS framework for Grade 4 mathematics

Content domain	Attributes		Times specified
Number	**Whole Numbers**		
	1. Represent, compare, and order whole numbers as well as demonstrating knowledge of place value.	Whole Number (1)	6
	2. Recognize multiples, computing with whole numbers using the four operations, and estimating computations.	Whole Number (2)	16
	3. Solve problems, including those set in real-life contexts (for example, measurement and money problems).	Whole Number (3)	11
	4. Solve problems involving proportions.	Whole Number (4)	3
	Fractions and Decimals		
	5. Recognize, represent, and understand fractions and decimals as parts of a whole and their equivalents.	Fractions & Decimals (1)	3
	6. Solve problems involving simple fractions and decimals including their addition and subtraction.	Fractions & Decimals (2)	2
	Number Sentences with Whole Numbers		
	7. Find the missing number or operation and model simple situations involving unknowns in number sentences or expressions.	Number Sentences	2
	Patterns and Relationships		
	8. Describe relationships in patterns and their extensions; generate pairs of whole numbers by a given rule and identify a rule for every relationship given pairs of whole numbers.	Patterns & Relationships	3
Geometric Shapes & Measurement	**Lines and Angles**		
	9. Measure, estimate, and understand properties of lines and angles and be able to draw them.	Lines & Angles	3
	Two- and Three-dimensional Shapes		
	10. Classify, compare, and recognize geometric figures and shapes and their relationships and elementary properties.	Two- & Three-dimensional Shapes (1)	7
	11. Calculate and estimate perimeters, area, and volume.	Two- & Three-dimensional Shapes (2)	2
	Location and Movement		
	12. Locate points in an informal coordinate to recognize and draw figures and their movement.	Location & Movement	3
Data & Display	**Reading and Interpreting**		
	13. Read data from tables, pictographs, bar graphs, and pie charts.	Reading & Interpreting (1)	4
	14. Compare and understand how to use information from data.	Reading & Interpreting (2)	3
	Organizing and Representing		
	15. Understand different representations and organize data using tables, pictographs, and bar graphs.	Organizing & Representing	2

Note: The bold headings in the attributes column designate the topic areas within the content domains as indicated by the TIMSS framework (Mullis et al., 2005).

The item in Figure 2 asked students how many more girls are in Class A than in Class B. Although students would have used various methods to solve this item, the dominant strategy validated by experts was coded into the Q-matrix. To solve this item, a student would need to be able to read and compare the proportions between boys and girls in Class A to infer that three-quarters of the students are girls. Because there are 40 students in Class A, students should also be able to deduce that there are 30 girls. For Class B, students would need to be able to read the bar graph and to understand that there are 16 girls. Finally, by determining the difference between 30 and 16, students should arrive at the correct answer, 14.

Correctly solving the problem associated with this item required mastery of six important attributes:

- *Attribute 1:* representing, comparing, and ordering whole numbers as well as demonstrating knowledge of place value;
- *Attribute 2:* recognizing multiples, computing with whole numbers by using the four operations, and estimating computations;
- *Attribute 5:* recognizing, representing, and understanding fractions and decimals as parts of a whole and their equivalents;
- *Attribute 6:* solving problems involving simple fractions and decimals, including their addition and subtraction;
- *Attribute 13:* reading data from tables, pictographs, bar graphs, and pie charts; and
- *Attribute 14:* comparing and understanding how to use information from data.

Table 3 shows the Q-matrix used for the current analysis. Because the validity of the Q-matrix rests on the content mastery and experience of the coders who develop it, we had three mathematics educators independently score our initial Q-matrix. We also asked two professionals with college-level mathematics training and experience in the field to complete the same exercise. We then, through a discussion and consensus process centered on the dominant method used to solve the item, combined the coding of the three Q-matrices to finalize the matrix that we used in this study.

The finalized Q-matrix formed the building block of our analysis, and its accuracy, as just implied, holds the validity of the findings of this study. Although, with respect to educational measurement, the implementation and application of a Q-matrix within a cognitive diagnostic modeling framework relates, to some degree, to what we discuss here, it is different in that we measured the clustering and association of attributes and not their prevalence or the classification of student mastery of a specific attribute.

In cognitive diagnostic models, use of a Q-matrix with 15 attributes and 25 items may require additional complexities in estimation (see Haberman & von Davier, 2006; von Davier 2005) because the latent trait space needed to classify individual students for a model with 15 attributes would contain 2^{15} different attribute mastery types. It is important to understand the difference between the cluster-based approach that essentially "explains" the correlations between the 15 sum scores used in our analysis

Table 3: Q-matrix for TIMSS 2007 Grade 4 mathematics test items

Item	Number (N)								Geometric shapes and measures				Data and display (DD)		
	1	2	3	4	5	6	7	8	9	10	11	12	13	14	15
1	1	1	0	0	0	0	0	0	0	0	0	0	0	0	0
2	0	0	0	0	1	0	0	0	0	0	0	0	0	0	0
3	0	1	0	1	1	0	0	0	0	0	0	0	0	0	0
4	0	0	1	0	0	1	0	0	0	0	0	0	0	0	0
5	0	1	1	0	0	0	0	1	0	0	0	0	0	0	0
6	0	0	0	0	0	0	0	0	0	1	0	1	0	0	0
7	0	0	0	0	0	0	0	0	1	1	0	1	0	0	0
8	1	1	1	0	0	0	0	0	0	1	1	0	0	0	0
9	0	0	0	0	0	0	0	0	0	1	0	0	0	0	0
10	0	0	0	0	0	0	0	0	1	1	0	0	0	0	0
11	0	1	1	1	0	0	0	0	1	0	0	0	0	0	0
12	1	0	0	0	0	0	0	0	0	0	0	0	1	0	1
13	1	1	0	1	0	0	0	0	0	0	0	0	1	0	0
14	1	1	0	0	1	1	0	0	0	0	0	0	1	1	0
15	0	1	1	0	0	0	0	0	0	0	0	0	0	0	0
16	0	1	1	0	0	0	0	0	0	0	0	0	0	0	0
17	0	1	0	0	0	0	1	0	0	0	0	0	0	0	0
18	0	1	1	0	0	0	0	1	0	0	0	0	0	0	0
19	0	1	1	0	0	0	0	0	0	0	0	0	0	1	0
20	0	1	1	0	0	0	0	1	0	0	0	0	0	1	0
21	0	1	1	0	0	0	1	0	0	0	0	0	0	0	0
22	0	0	0	0	0	0	0	0	0	1	1	1	0	0	0
23	0	1	1	0	0	0	0	0	0	0	0	0	0	0	0
24	0	0	0	0	0	0	0	0	0	1	0	0	0	0	0
25	1	1	0	0	0	0	0	0	0	0	0	0	1	0	1

with a low number of (two to three) clusters and the model for individual cognitive diagnosis utilized to classify individual respondents into multiple binary mastery or ordered attributes.

Analysis

To conduct a cluster analysis of attributes based on examinee performance, we combined the examinees' item response data (Y_{ij}) with the Q-matrix (q_{jk}) developed for the study (see Table 3) via the sum-score vector method. The resulting examinee-by-attribute sum-score matrix, W_{ik}, represents a combination of the summed item responses to the 15 attributes specified in the Q-matrix; in other words, it gives examinees a score for each of the 15 attributes. As such, we could assume that test-takers with a higher score in the W_{ik} matrix would be the test-takers most likely to have the attribute specified in the Q-matrix.

Using the sum-score matrix W_{ik}, we then used Euclidian distances to create a matrix of dissimilarities. (The Euclidian measure tends to be the default choice of distance measure for most cluster analyses.) We used the matrix dissimilarity command in Stata 10 (StataCorp, 2007) to do this. This command offers a flexible syntax by which to create and modify different types of similarity and dissimilarity matrices.

Our next step required us to use the procedure described above to create a separate dissimilarities matrix for the 11 regions (i.e., the nine countries and the two American states). We then used the dissimilarities matrices to conduct the cluster analysis. Because the K-means cluster method requires a prespecified number of clusters, we calculated the fusion coefficient for each cluster and its confidence intervals (Aldenderfer & Blashfield, 1984; Wishart, 2005) for each region and examined these in order to determine the largest gap (i.e., the elbow in the scree plots depicted in the results section below). Although this measure can be subjective, it provided us with an arbitrary starting point for the number of clusters. We again used Stata 10 (StataCorp, 2007) to conduct the K-means and HACA analyses and a PASCAL-based EXTREE program (Corter & Tversky, 1986) to run the EXTREE analysis.

RESULTS

Because we selected the 11 regions on the basis of their students' overall performance (i.e., each region's mean proficiency score), the magnitude of the derived distance measures reflected attribute dissimilarities: better-performing countries had larger dissimilarity indices. At the same time, the values in the dissimilarity matrix may have been affected by the variation in the attribute specification of the Q-matrix; thus, test-takers needed to draw on some attributes more frequently than others, as shown in Table 3. As such, the number of times an attribute was required, which ranged from 2 to 16 times, could also have changed the dissimilarity matrix.

Hong Kong (ranked first on the international TIMMS achievement scale) had the highest values for each cell of the matrix because we used the sum-score vector to calculate each value. Likewise, Yemen, which ranked 43rd on the international scale, had the poorest-performing students and the lowest dissimilarity indices. As we noted earlier, the dissimilarities represent further distance in space and so are less related to one another. Although the overall performance implied the variability of the distances, they did not necessarily infer that the distances would be strictly greater for a better performing country over another country of lower performance. This is because the presence or the absence of a required attribute in the Q-matrix influences the outcome of the dissimilarity matrix.

To determine the number of clusters assigned for the K-means analysis, we used the fusion coefficient to generate a plot that would allow us to examine where the greatest difference occurred. Figure 3 shows this result for one region, the United States. Here we can see that the elbow of the coefficient is formed of three clusters. Although we created fusion coefficients for each country, the elbow of the coefficient for most of the selected regions was made up of three clusters. Because the number of clusters formed by using the fusion coefficient can be the product of subjectivity, we selected three clusters that we could use uniformly for all countries. This meant that we could summarize the differences between test-takers on the 15 attribute scores in terms of their membership with respect to one of these three clusters. We then used these in the *K*-means analyses to explain the dependencies between the 15 scores developed from the Q-matrix generated by the mathematics educators and experts.

Figure 3: Plot of fusion coefficients

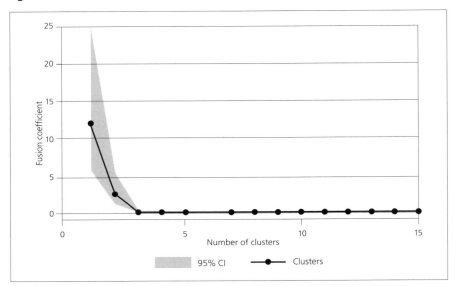

Tables 4, 5, and 6 present the results of the *K*-means clusters for the high-, average-, and low-performing regions, respectively. Table 4 shows the clusters for Hong Kong, Chinese Taipei, Massachusetts, and Minnesota.

The three clusters for *Hong Kong* were as follows:

- *Cluster One:* Attributes 1, 2, and 3 (whole numbers 1, 2, and 3, number domain) and Attribute 10 (two- and three-dimensional shapes 1, geometric shapes and measurement domain) grouped within Cluster 1;

- *Cluster Two:* Attributes 5 (fractions and decimals 1, number domain), 8 (patterns and relationships, number domain), 12 (location and movement, geometric shapes and measurement domain), 13 (reading and interpreting 1, data and display domain), 14 (reading and interpreting 2, data and display domain), and 15 (organizing and representing, data and display domain);

- *Cluster Three:* Attributes 4 (whole number 4, number domain), 6 (fractions and decimals 2, number domain), 7 (number sentences, number domain), 9 (lines and angles, geometric shapes and measurement domain), and 11 (two- and three-dimensional shapes 2, geometric shapes and measurement domain).

Table 4: *K*-means clustering for high-performing regions

	Cluster 1	Cluster 2	Cluster 3
Hong Kong (Rank #1)	Whole Number (1) Whole Number (2) Whole Number (3) 2- & 3-D Shapes (1)	Fraction & Decimal (1) Patterns & Relations Location & Movement Reading & Interpreting (1) Reading & Interpreting (2) Organizing & Representing	Whole Number (4) Fraction & Decimal (2) Number Sentences Lines & Angles 2- & 3-D Shapes (2)
Chinese Taipei (Rank #3)	Whole Number (1) 2- & 3-D Shapes (1) Reading & Interpreting (1)	Whole Number (2) Whole Number (3)	Whole Number (4) Fraction & Decimal (1) Fraction & Decimal (2) Number Sentences Patterns & Relations Lines & Angles 2- & 3-D Shapes (2) Location & Movement Reading & Interpreting (2) Organizing & Representing
Massachusetts (Rank #4)	Whole Number (1) 2- & 3-D Shapes (1) Reading & Interpreting (1)	Whole Number (2) Whole Number (3)	Whole Number (4) Fraction & Decimal (1) Fraction & Decimal (2) Number Sentences Patterns & Relations Lines & Angles 2- & 3-D Shapes (2) Location & Movement Reading & Interpreting (2) Organizing & Representing
Minnesota (Rank #6)	Whole Number (1) 2- & 3-D Shapes (1) Reading & Interpreting (1)	Whole Number (2) Whole Number (3)	Whole Number (4) Fraction & Decimal (1) Fraction & Decimal (2) Number Sentences Patterns & Relations Lines & Angles 2- & 3-D Shapes (2) Location & Movement Reading & Interpreting (2) Organizing & Representing

Note: Chinese Taipei, Massachusetts, and Minnesota have the same attributes.

Chinese Taipei and the participating regional entities of *Massachusetts* and *Minnesota* (see Table 5) shared the same clusters:

- *Cluster 1:* Attributes 1 (whole number 1, number domain), 10 (two- and three-dimensional shapes 1, geometric shapes and measurement domain), and 13 (reading and interpreting 1, data and display domain);

- *Cluster 2:* Attributes 2 and 3 (whole number 2 and 3, number domain);

- *Cluster 3:* all remaining attributes. This cluster thus contained all attributes from the geometric shapes and measurement domain and the two remaining attributes from the data and display domain.

With respect to the average-performing countries (Table 5), the structure of the attribute clusters for the *United States* and *Sweden* (Table 5) replicated the structure for *Chinese Taipei*, *Massachusetts*, and *Minnesota*. However, for *Denmark*, Attributes

1, 2, and 3 (whole numbers 1, 2, and 3, number domain) and 10 (two- and three-dimensional shapes 1, geometric shapes and measurement domain) grouped into Cluster One. This cluster contained the same attributes that comprised Cluster One for *Hong Kong*.

The attributes in Cluster Two—Attributes 12 (location and movement, geometric shapes and measurement domain), 13 (reading and interpreting 1, data and display domain), and 15 (organizing and representing, data and display domain)—were also found in *Hong Kong's* Cluster Two. Although the remaining attributes fell into Cluster Three, the classifications of attributes in *Denmark* and in *Hong Kong* were similar.

Table 5: *K*-means clustering for average-performing regions

	Cluster 1	Cluster 2	Cluster 3
United States (Rank #13)	Whole Number (1) 2- & 3-D Shapes (1) Reading & Interpreting (1)	Whole Number (2) Whole Number (3)	Whole Number (4) Fraction & Decimal (1) Fraction & Decimal (2) Number Sentences Patterns & Relations Lines & Angles 2- & 3-D Shapes (2) Location & Movement Reading & Interpreting (2) Organizing & Representing
Denmark (Rank #15)	Whole Number (1) Whole Number (2) Whole Number (3) 2- & 3-D Shapes (1)	Location & Movement Reading & Interpreting (1) Organizing & Representing	Whole Number (4) Fractions & Decimals (1) Fractions & Decimals (2) Number Sentences Patterns & Relationships Lines & Angles 2- & 3-D Shapes (2) Reading & Interpreting (2)
Sweden (Rank #24)	Whole Number (1) 2- & 3-D Shapes (1) Reading & Interpreting (1)	Whole Number (2) Whole Number (3)	Whole Number (4) Fraction & Decimal (1) Fraction & Decimal (2) Number Sentences Patterns & Relations Lines & Angles 2- & 3-D Shapes (2) Location & Movement Reading & Interpreting (2) Organizing & Representing

Note: The United States and Sweden have the same attributes in the clusters.

Table 6 shows the *K*-means clusters for the four low-performing countries (Colombia, Kuwait, Qatar, and Yemen). Note that the attribute classifications for these countries differ from the ones presented earlier.

The three clusters for *Colombia* were as follows:

* *Cluster One:* Attributes 1 (whole number 1, number domain), 10 (two- and three-dimensional shapes, geometric shapes and measurement domain), 13 (reading and interpreting, data and display domain), and 15 (organizing and representing, data and display domain);

Table 6: *K*-means clustering for low-performing regions

	Cluster 1	Cluster 2	Cluster 3
Colombia (Rank #37)	Whole Number (1) 2- & 3-D Shapes (1) Reading & Interpreting (1) Organizing & Representing	Whole Number (2) Whole Number (3)	Whole Number (4) Fractions & Decimals (1) Fractions & Decimals (2) Number Sentences Patterns & Relationships Lines & Angles 2- & 3-D Shapes (2) Location & Movement Reading & Interpreting (2)
Kuwait (Rank #41)	Whole Number (1) Whole Number (2) Whole Number (3) 2- & 3-D Shapes (1)	Fractions & Decimals (1) Fractions & Decimals (2) Number Sentences	Whole Number (4) Patterns & Relationships Lines & Angles 2- & 3-D Shapes (2) Location & Movement Reading & Interpreting (1) Reading & Interpreting (2) Organizing & Representing
Qatar (Rank #42)	Whole Number (1) Whole Number (2) Whole Number (3) 2- & 3-D Shapes (1)	Patterns & Relationships 2- & 3-D Shapes (2) Location & Movement Reading & Interpreting (1)	Whole Number (4) Fractions & Decimals (1) Fractions & Decimals (2) Number Sentences Lines & Angles 2- & 3-D Shapes (2) Reading & Interpreting (2)
Yemen (Rank #43)	Whole Number (1) Whole Number (3) 2- & 3-D Shapes (1)	Whole Number (2)	Whole Number (4) Fraction & Decimal (1) Fraction & Decimal (2) Number Sentences Patterns & Relations Lines & Angles 2- & 3-D Shapes (2) Location & Movement Reading & Interpreting (1) Reading & Interpreting (2) Organizing & Representing

- *Cluster Two:* Attributes 2 and 3 (whole number 2 and 3, number domain);
- *Cluster Three:* all remaining attributes.

The first cluster for *Kuwait* and for *Qatar* were similar in that they both contained Attributes 1, 2, and 3 (whole numbers 1, 2, and 3, number domain) and Attribute 10 (two- and three-dimensional shapes, geometric shapes and measurement domain). However, Clusters Two and Three for these two regions differed. The Cluster Two attributes for Kuwait were from the number domain, namely Attributes 5 and 6 (fractions and decimals 1 and 2), and 7 (number sentences). For *Qatar*, the Cluster Two attributes contained attributes from the number, geometric shapes and measurement, and data and display domains.

The Cluster One attributes for the final country—*Yemen*—comprised Attributes 1 and 3 (whole number 1 and 3, number domain) and 10 (two- and three-dimensional shapes, geometric shapes and measurement domain). The second cluster for *Yemen* contained only one attribute—Attribute 2 (whole number 2, number domain).

In general, we found differences in the classification of attributes across the 11 regions. However, the clusters across the higher-performing countries were more similar in structure than the clusters across the lower-performing countries.

Figures 4, 5, and 6 show the hierarchical clusters—derived from the HACA method via complete linkage—across the high-, average-, and low-performing countries, respectively. All of the dendrograms for the 11 regions show three main clusters, the hierarchical structures of which were similar to one another and resembled the results from the *K*-means analysis.

In 10 regions (the exception was *Kuwait*), one cluster comprised Attributes 2 and 3 (whole number 2 and 3, number domain); this is the right-most cluster on the dendrograms. The left-most cluster for the high- and average-performing countries (Hong Kong, *Chinese Taipei*, *Massachusetts*, *Minnesota*, the *United States*, *Denmark*, and *Sweden*) contained Attribute 1 (whole numbers 1, number domain), 10 (two- and three-dimensional shapes, geometric shapes and measurement domain), and 13 (reading and interpreting, data and display domain). The remaining attributes clustered into two subgroups comprising attributes from the number, geometric shapes and measures, and data and display domains. The hierarchical clusters that emerged from the low-performing countries showed differences for the far-left cluster (Figure 6). *Colombia's* HACA, for example, had five attributes, while *Kuwait's* had four.

Figure 4: Hierarchical agglomerative cluster dendrogram for high-performing regions

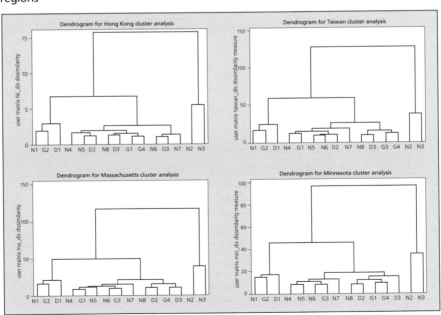

Figure 5: Hierarchical agglomerative cluster dendrogram for average-performing regions

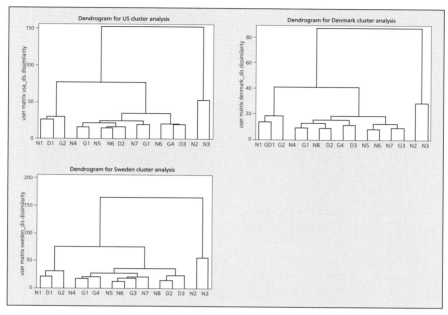

Figure 6: Hierarchical agglomerative cluster dendrogram for low-performing regions

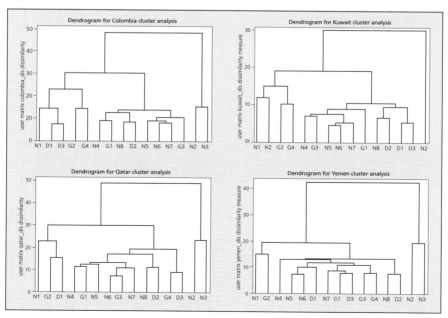

Note: N = number domain, G = geometric shapes and measures domain, D = data and display domain.

We used the results from both the *K*-means and the HACA clusters to conduct the EXTREE analysis. Table 7 shows the fit statistics derived from running the EXTREE procedure. The proportion of variance accounted for by each dataset was approximately or above 99%, and the stress statistics were between good to excellent, with these ratings based on Borg and Groenen's (2005) recommendations. These indicators thus showed that the EXTREE model had a good fit with the data.

Table 7: Fit statistics

Rank	Fit statistic	Stress formula 1	Stress formula 2	*R*(monotonic) squared	*R*-squared (p.v.a.f.)*
1	Hong Kong	0.035	0.053	0.997	0.994
3	Chinese Taipei	0.021	0.032	0.999	0.999
4	Massachusetts	0.025	0.039	0.999	0.997
6	Minnesota	0.026	0.042	0.998	0.997
13	USA	0.030	0.050	0.998	0.995
15	Denmark	0.034	0.058	0.997	0.997
24	Sweden	0.031	0.050	0.998	0.997
37	Colombia	0.031	0.064	0.996	0.991
41	Kuwait	0.039	0.092	0.992	0.978
42	Qatar	0.038	0.090	0.992	0.983
43	Yemen	0.032	0.064	0.996	0.987

Notes:
Stress values less than 0.050 are considered good fit, and values less than 0.025 are considered excellent fit (Borg & Groenen, 2005).
*Proportion of variance accounted for.

Figures 7, 8, and 9 show the hierarchical clusters produced by the EXTREE model for the high-, average-, and low-performing regions, respectively. The cluster structures that emerged from the EXTREE analysis were similar to those that emerged from the *K*-means and HACA analyses. The following presents the attributes grouped within the EXTREE clusters for the three groups of countries.

- *High-performing regions* (Figure 7): a single hierarchical cluster emerged that contained Attributes 1, 2, and 3 (whole number 1, 2, and 3, number domain), 10 (two- and three-dimensional shapes 1, geometric shapes and measurement domain), and 13 (reading and interpreting 1, data and display domain). However, there were variations in this cluster. For example, in *Hong Kong*, *Massachusetts*, and *Minnesota*, Attribute 15 (organizing and representing, data and display domain) was included in the hierarchical cluster. A secondary cluster also seems to have formed in *Chinese Taipei* and *Minnesota*.

- *Average-performing regions* (Figure 8): here we observed a distinct second hierarchical cluster that included Attributes 1, 2, 3, 10, 13, and 15. We also noted a secondary cluster that included Attributes 4 (whole number 4, number domain), 5 and 6 (fractions and decimals 1 and 2, number domain), 7 (number sentences, number domain), and 11 (two- and three-dimensional shapes 2, geometric shapes and measurement domain). The hierarchical clusters for *Denmark* and the *United States* also included Attribute 14 (reading and interpreting, data and display domain), and for *Sweden*, included Attribute 9 (lines and angles, geometric shapes and measurement domain).

- *Low-performing regions* (Figure (9): the cluster pattern for these regions was similar to the patterns for both the high- and average-performing regions; the cluster formed from Attributes 1, 2, 3, and 10 was also present for this last grouping but with additional attributes. We also observed a hierarchical cluster formed by Attributes 5, 6, 7, and 11 for *Colombia*, *Kuwait*, and *Qatar*. Although we noted variations in the attribute clusters across the low-performing regions, the hierarchical structure of these clusters varied little from the structure of the average-performing regions.

Figure 7: Extended similarities tree dendrograms for high-performing regions

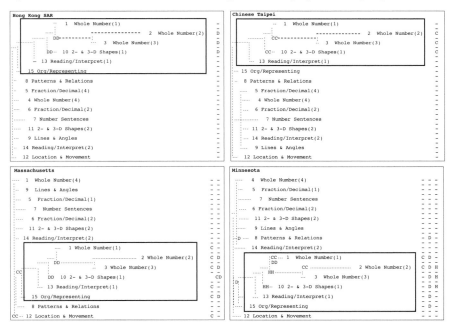

Tables 8, 9, and 10 present the overlapping clusters that were also generated by the EXTREE model for the high-, average-, and low-performing regions, respectively. The most prominent outcome of this analysis was the number of clusters associated with the regions' respective rankings on the TIMSS international achievement scale. The tables show that the regions of lower performance had more overlapping clusters. *Hong Kong* and *Chinese Taipei* had one, *Massachusetts* two, *Minnesota* three, and the *United States* four. Both *Denmark* and *Sweden* had five attributes.

Figure 8: Extended similarities tree dendrograms for average-performing regions

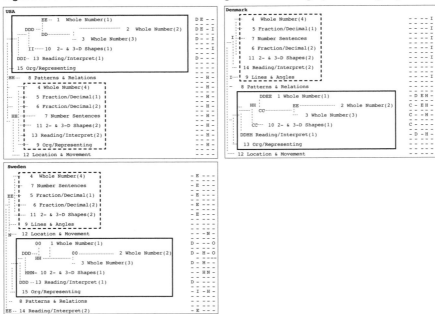

Figure 9: Extended similarities tree dendrograms for low-performing regions

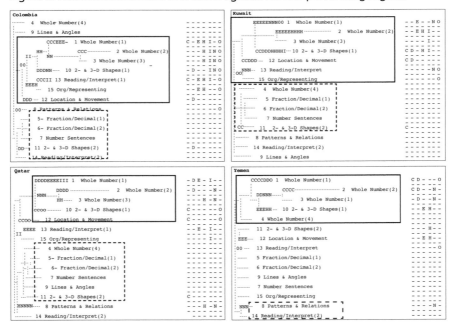

Table 8: Overlapping features for high-performing regions

Region	Overlapping features						
	1	2	3	4	5	6	7
Hong Kong (Rank #1)	Whole Number (2) Whole Number (3) 2-&3-D Shapes (1)						
Chinese Taipei (Rank #3)	Whole Number (2) Whole Number (3) 2-&3-D Shapes (1)						
Massachusetts (Rank #4)	Whole Number (2) Whole Number (2) Whole Number (3) 2-&3-D Shapes (1) 2- & 3- D Shapes (1)	Whole Number (1) Whole Number (1) Whole Number (2) Whole Number (3) Location & Movement Reading & Interpreting (1) Organizing & Representing					
Minnesota (Rank #6)	Whole Number (2) Whole Number (3) 2- & 3-D Shapes (1) 2- & 3- D Shapes (1)	Whole Number (1) Whole Number (2) Whole Number (3) Patterns & Relations Reading & Interpreting (1) Organizing & Representing	Whole Number (1) Whole Number (2)				

Note: Hong Kong and Chinese Taipei have the same overlapping clusters, as do Massachusetts and Minnesota.

Table 9: Overlapping features for average-performing regions

Region	Overlapping features						
	1	2	3	4	5	6	7
United States (Rank #13)	Whole Number (1) Whole Number (1) Whole Number (2)	Whole Number (4) Whole Number (3) 2- & 3- D Shapes (1) Reading & Interpreting (1)	Whole Number (2) Whole Number (3) Whole Number (1)	Number Sentences Fraction & Decimal (1) Fraction & Decimal (2) Lines & Angles 2- & 3- D Shapes (2) Patterns & Relations Reading & Interpreting (2)	Whole Number (4) Fraction & Decimal (1) Fraction & Decimal (2) Number Sentences 2- & 3-D Shapes (2) Lines & Angles		
Denmak (Rank #15)	Whole Number (1) Whole Number (2)	Whole Number (2) Whole Number (3) 2- & 3-D Shapes (1)	Whole Number (1) Whole Number (2) Whole Number (3) Reading & Interpreting (1)	Whole Number (1) Reading & Interpreting (1)			
Sweden (Rank #24)	Whole Number (1) Whole Number (2)	Whole Number (2) Whole Number (3) 2- & 3-D Shapes (1)	Whole Number (1) Whole Number (2) Whole Number (3) Reading & Interpreting (1)	2- & 3-D Shapes (1) Location & Movement	Whole Number (4) Fraction & Decimal (1) Fraction & Decimal (2) Number Sentences 2- & 3-D Shapes (2) Reading & Interpreting (2) Organizing & Representing		

Note: Clusters with the same overlapping attributes across the different regions are marked to emphasize the prevalence of similar features.

Table 10: Overlapping features for low-performing regions

Region	Overlapping features						
	1	2	3	4	5	6	7
Colombia (Rank #37)	Whole Number (1) Whole Number (2) Reading & Interpreting (1)	Whole Number (2) Whole Number (3) 2- & 3-D Shapes (1)	2- & 3-D Shapes (1) 2- & 3-D Shapes (2) Location & Movement	Whole Number (1) Reading & Interpreting (1) Organizing & Representing	Whole Number (1) Whole Number (2) Whole Number (3) Reading & Interpreting (1) Organizing & Representing	Whole Number (1) Whole Number (2) Whole Number (3) Reading & Interpreting (1) 2- & 3-D Shapes (1)	Whole Number (1) Whole Number (2) Whole Number (3) 2- & 3-D Shapes (1) Reading & Interpreting (1) Organizing & Representing (1) Patterns & Relations
Kuwait (Rank #41)	Whole Number (1) Whole Number (1) Whole Number (2)	Whole Number (2) Whole Number (2) Whole Number (3) 2- & 3-D Shapes (1)	2-&3-DShapes (1) 2-&3-DShapes (1) 2-&3-DShapes (2) Location & Movement	Whole Number (1) Whole Number (1) Reading & Interpreting (1) Organizing & Representing	Whole Number (1) Whole Number (1) Reading & Interpreting (1)	2- & 3-D Shapes (1) Location & Movement	Whole Number (2) 2- & 3-D Shapes (1)
Qatar (Rank #42)	Whole Number (1) Whole Number (2)	Whole Number (2) Whole Number (3) Patterns & Relations	2- & 3-D Shapes (1) 2- & 3-D Shapes (2) Location & Movement	Whole Number (1) Reading & Interpreting (1) Organizing & Representing	Whole Number (1) Reading & Interpreting (1)	2- & 3-D Shapes (1) Location & Movement	Whole Number (3) Patterns & Relations
Yemen (Rank #43)	Whole Number (1) Whole Number (2)	Whole Number (2) Whole Number (3) Patterns & Relations	2- & 3- D Shapes (1) 2- & 3- D Shapes (2) Location & Movement	Whole Number (1) Whole Number (2) Whole Number (3)	Whole Number (1) Reading & Interpreting (1)	2- & 3- D Shapes (1) Location & Movement	

Note: Clusters with the same overlapping attributes across the different regions are marked to emphasize the prevalence of similar features.

Seven overlapping clusters were evident among the low-performing regions (Table 10). *Colombia*, *Kuwait*, and *Qatar* had seven such clusters, while *Yemen*, the lowest-ranking region, had six. Unlike the patterns evident in the previous tables and figures, the attributes presented in Table 10 did not distinctly group in only one cluster. In other words, the same attribute appeared in more than one cluster, which was not surprising given the clusters represented overlapping attributes. Similar to the results shown previously, Attributes 2 (whole number 2, number domain), 3 (whole number 3, number domain), and 10 (two- and three-dimensional shapes 1, geometric shapes and measurement domain) formed one cluster for *Hong Kong*, *Chinese Taipei*, *Massachusetts*, *Minnesota*, the *United States*, *Denmark*, *Sweden*, *Colombia*, and *Kuwait*. Attributes 1 and 2 (whole number 1 and 2, number domain) also formed a cluster for *Minnesota*, the *United States*, *Denmark*, *Kuwait*, *Qatar*, and *Yemen*.

Of the two benchmarking participants, *Massachusetts* had two clusters. *Minnesota*, however, had these same two clusters and one other. The overlapping clusters for *Denmark* and *Sweden* were similar in that the attributes in four out of five of the clusters were the same. We also noted overlapping clusters that were present only among the low-performing regions. For example, in all four regions, Attributes 10 and 11 (two- and three-dimensional shapes 1 and 2, geometric shapes and measurement domain) and 12 (location and movement, geometric shapes and measurement domain) overlapped (see Cluster Three) and were from the geometric shapes and measurement domain. Again, Attributes 1 (whole number 1, number domain), 13 (reading and interpreting, data and display domain), and 15 (organizing and representing, data and display domain) were all present within the four regions. Furthermore, for *Kuwait*, *Qatar*, and *Yemen*, Attributes 1 and 13 overlapped, as did attributes 10 and 12 (see Clusters 5 and 6). Again, given the overlapping nature of the clusters, the presence of an attribute in more than one cluster shows that the attribute is not distinct and that it is less hierarchical.

DISCUSSION AND CONCLUSION

Our purpose in conducting this study was to identify, from the TIMSS Grade 4 mathematics test items, patterns of attribute clusters. We used the distances presented by the accuracy of student responses to generate a dissimilarity proximity matrix. We observed, with respect to the 25 items and 15 attributes that we selected for this study, a common pattern emerging from the hierarchical clusters and overlapping features.

When conducting our analyses, we used clustered attributes, a focus that differs from previous studies of clustering within the context of cognitive diagnosis, where the researchers concerned examined items (see, for example, Beller, 1990; Corter, 1995; Sireci & Geisinger, 1992) or examinees (e.g., Chiu et al., 2009; Chiu & Seo, 2009). The findings of these studies and ours nevertheless show that clusters tend to vary across items, examinees, and attributes, depending on the application. As such, this study provides a framework for examining structures of attribute clusters that may help researchers and policymakers not only view, from a macroscopic perspective, how students demonstrate their mastery of attributes, but also gain some idea of how students determine which attributes to use.

Our results also show that there is considerable value in examining the cluster structures produced by the K-means and the HACA, and that these analyses can be usefully extended to the EXTREE model, which, in our case, supported the cluster structures of the former two methods. We noted from the dissimilarity matrix that a region with higher performance also had greater measures of distance, meaning that an attribute was further apart in space. This was generally the case for the higher-performing regions both cross-nationally and within the United States. Furthermore, the findings from these cluster analyses suggest that Attributes 1 (whole numbers 1, number domain), 2 (whole numbers 2, number domain), 3 (whole numbers 3, number domain), 10 (two- and three-dimensional shapes 1, geometric shapes and measurement domain), and also 13 (reading and interpreting 1, data and display domain) would continue to cluster. The fact that this pattern emerged from all three methods both across and within all regions suggests a common skill derived from whole numbers, two- and three-dimensional shapes, and reading and interpreting data. We suspect this pattern was indeed the case with respect to our analyses, because the application of whole numbers constituted a wide range of joint usage with other attributes.

When examining the cluster structures across regions, we found a greater degree of similarity with respect to attribute classification across the higher- and average-performing regions than across the lower-performing regions. The K-means results revealed that Hong Kong had a greater distribution of attribute classification than any other country, while the United States and its two benchmarking states had the same classifications. We noted the same pattern within the results of the HACA, with attributes in the lower-performing regions being the most different in structure. However, the three retained clusters were quite similar to one another.

The outcomes of the EXTREE analysis, which simultaneously combined the hierarchical and overlapping attributes, showed that the poorer a region's performance, the higher the incidence of attribute clusters. Thus, higher numbers of clusters and classification of attributes into multiple clusters, as indicated by the overlapping clusters, were most evident among the lower-performing countries. Although the hierarchical structures within the United States and in Massachusetts and Minnesota were similar, the overlapping clusters showed that even within the United States differences could be observed intra-nationally.

We consider that the greatest value in conducting our cluster analysis resided in the opportunity it gave us to examine the overlapping clusters of attributes, especially in terms of whether students in a particular region perceived and processed a specific attribute with reference to or in the same way as another attribute. Although the analysis conducted in this study was exploratory, in that one cannot fully claim the clustering of attributes to imply a low mastery of a particular skill, the consistency in the patterns is notable. Furthermore, the clustering of attributes also indicates that attributes tend to be learned together, a happenstance that may be the product of various cognitive, developmental, and/or curriculum factors. Yet, given the assumption that the 15 attributes that we used in our study were distinct and separately used for solving problems, the results may lead to useful indicators for researchers and instructors. The clearer attribute structures and performance patterns of the higher-performing countries may thus be due to these countries having more standardized curricula, or their students having better basic skills.

In the case of the lower-performing regions (Colombia, Kuwait, Qatar, and Yemen)—the regions with the most overlapping clusters—the lack of clearly differentiated clusters makes it difficult to identify them as having distinct and unique attribute structures. Instructors can, however, take this information to identify the grouped clusters with the aim of separating out the overlapping structures of these clusters. In the two American states that we included in order to evaluate the cluster structure within the same country, there seemed to be both disparities and similarities in the clusters. We again emphasize at this point that the appearance of overlapping clusters in low-performing regions does not necessarily mean that the cluster structure is less distinct, but rather that the structure is less hierarchical. We consider that more study directed at examining the relationship between overlapping clusters and student mastery of attributes is needed.

Our study presented another advantage associated with examining clusters of attributes. This was a reduction in the computational burden arising out of traditional techniques of cluster analysis. Unlike other models of cognitive diagnosis that use restricted latent classes for classification and therefore require heavy computational power, all analyses conducted in this study can be run using most statistical software packages under their usual running speeds (i.e., fewer than three seconds for all convergence when using standard computing memory and processors). Once again, we need to note that the models we used included cluster attributes, not students. Therefore, researchers interested in investigating or exploring the cluster structures of attributes to determine preliminary results should find the method presented in this paper an efficient way to examine how students tend to draw on the multiple attributes assumed relevant for solving mathematics problems. This type of exploratory work can furthermore aid the creation and validation of the Q-matrix, especially given that this method does, at times, involve a cumbersome process. The clustering information provided by an analysis such as this can furthermore be used as diagnostic feedback with respect to construction of that analysis. It can also be used to help identify different cognitive diagnosis models useful for describing the structure of the attributes.

In short, the main finding of this study indicates that clustering methods, especially those using EXTREE, can be useful for detecting the overlapping clusters that other clustering methods do not show; perhaps they may indicate areas that low-performing students can focus on in order to improve their achievement. This is another area that requires further research. Although the results that emerged from our K-means and HACA analyses were similar, the clusters formed by EXTREE provided a greater depth of information. This outcome may indicate that students from higher-performing regions have a greater applied understanding of the attributes needed to solve a particular item-based problem because they perceive and use these attributes as distinct and independent from others. The tendency toward clustering of both similar and unrelated attributes evident in the lower-performing countries likely indicates student uncertainty and a lack of mastery of the required attributes. Utilization of the fine-grained attributes specified in this analysis can therefore not only help improve student performance, but also serve as a reliable method for sorting and providing achievement-based information of a kind that educational researchers and policymakers will find most useful. For these individuals, opportunity to examine and tease out the attributes within overlapping clusters should help them focus more effectively on the specific areas of learning identified as necessary to improve students' mastery and understanding of when to apply a particular attribute.

References

Aldenderfer, M. S., & Blashfield, R. K. (1984). *Cluster analysis*. Newbury Park, CA: Sage.

Beller, M. (1990). Tree versus geometric representation of tests and items. *Applied Psychological Measurement*, *14*(1), 13–28.

Birenbaum, M., Tatsuoka, C., & Yamada, Y. (2004, May). *Diagnostic assessment in TIMMS-R: Comparison of eighth graders' mathematics knowledge states in the United States, Japan, and Israel*. Paper presented at the First IEA International Research Conference Lefkosia, Cyprus. Retrieved from http://www.iea.nl/fileadmin/user_upload/IRC2004/ Birenbaum_ Tatsuoka_Yamada.pdf

Borg, I., & Groenen, P. (2005). *Modern multidimensional scaling: Theory and applications* (2nd ed.). New York, NY: Springer-Verlag.

Cai, J. (2007). What is effective mathematics teaching? A study of teachers from Australia, Mainland China, Hong Kong, and the United States. *Mathematics Education*, *39*, 265–270.

Cai, J., & Silver, E. A. (1995). Solution processes and interpretations of solutions in solving a division-with-remainder story problem: Do Chinese and U.S. students have similar difficulties? *Journal for Research in Mathematics Education*, *26*, 491–497.

Chen, Y.-H., Gorin, J. S., Thompson, M. S., & Tatsuoka, K. K. (2008). Cross-cultural validity of the TIMSS-1999 mathematics test: Verification of a cognitive model. *International Journal of Testing*, *8*, 251–271.

Chiu, C., Douglas, J., & Li, X. (2009). Cluster analysis for cognitive diagnosis: Theory and applications. *Psychometrika*, *74*, 633–665.

Chiu, C., & Seo, M. (2009). Cluster analysis for cognitive diagnosis: An application to the 2001 PIRLS reading assessment. *IERI Monograph Series: Issues and Methodologies in Large-Scale Assessments*, *2*, 137–159.

Corter, J. E. (1995). Using clustering methods to explore the structure of diagnostic tests. In P. Nichols, S. Chipman, & R. Brennan (Eds.), *Cognitively diagnostic assessment* (pp. 305–326). Hillsdale, NJ: Lawrence Erlbaum Associates.

Corter, J. E., & Tversky, A. (1986). Extended similarity trees. *Psychometrika*, *51*, 429–451.

Dogan, E., & Tatsuoka, K. K. (2008). An international comparison using a diagnostic testing model: Turkish students' profile of mathematical skills on TIMSS-R. *Educational Studies in Mathematics*, *68*(3), 263–272.

Embretson, S. (1984). A general latent trait model for response processes. *Psychometrika*, *49*, 175–186.

Foy, P., & Olson, J. F. (2009). *TIMSS 2007 user guide for the international database*. Chestnut Hill, MA: Boston College.

Gierl, M. J. (2007). Making diagnostic inferences about cognitive attributes using the rule-space model and attribute hierarchy method. *Journal of Educational Measurement*, *44*(4), 325–340.

Givvin, K. B., Hiebert, J., Jacobs, J. K., Hollingsworth, H., & Gallimore, R. (2005). Are there national patterns of teaching? Evidence from the TIMSS 1999 video study. *Comparative Education Review*, *49*, 311–343.

Haberman, S. J., & von Davier, M. (2006). A note on models for cognitive diagnosis. In C. R. Rao & S. Sinharay (Eds.), *Handbook of statistics: Vol. 26. Psychometrics* (pp. 1031–1038). Amsterdam, the Netherlands: Elsevier.

Hair, J. F., Black, B., Babin, B., Anderson, R. E., & Tatham, R. L. (2006). *Multivariate data analysis* (6th ed). Upper Saddle River, NJ: Prentice Hall.

Hartigan, J. A. (1975). *Clustering algorithms*. New York, NY: Wiley.

Hiebert, J., Stigler, J. W., Jacobs, J. K., Givvin, K. B., Garnier, H., Smith, M., ... Gallimore, R. (2005). Mathematics teaching in the United States today (and tomorrow): Results from the TIMSS 1999 video study. *Educational Evaluation and Policy Analysis*, *27*, 111–132.

Hook, W., Bishop, W., & Hook, J. (2007). A quality math curriculum in support of effective teaching for elementary schools. *Educational Studies in Mathematics*, *65*, 125–148.

House, D. J. (2005). Motivational qualities of instructional strategies and computer use for mathematics teaching in Japan and the United States: Results from the TIMSS 1999 assessment. *International Journal of Instructional Media*, *32*, 89–105.

IES National Center for Education Statistics. (n. d.). *Trends in International Mathematics and Science Study (TIMSS)*. Washington, DC: Author. Retrieved from http://nces.ed.gov/timss/index.asp

Kuhs, T. M., & Ball, D. L. (1986). *Approaches to teaching mathematics: Mapping the domains of knowledge, skills, and dispositions* [Research memo]. East Lansing, MI: Michigan State University, Center on Teacher Education.

Lubienski, S. T. (2000). Problem solving as a means toward mathematics for all: An exploratory look through a class lens. *Journal for Research in Mathematics Education*, *31*, 454–482.

MacQueen, J. (1967). Some methods of classification and analysis of multivariate observations. In L. M. Le Cam & J. Neyman (Eds.), *Proceedings of the Fifth Berkeley Symposium on Mathematical Statistics and Probability* (pp. 281–207). Berkeley, CA: University of California Press.

McNeely, M. (Ed.). (1997). *Guidebook to examine school curricula*. Washington, DC: Office of Educational Research and Improvement, U.S. Department of Education.

Menon, P. (2000). Should the United States emulate Singapore's education system to achieve Singapore's success in the TIMSS? *Mathematics Teaching in the Middle School*, *5*, 345–348.

Mullis, I. V.S., Martin M. O., Ruddock, G. J., O'Sullivan, C. Y., Arora, A., & Erberber, E. (2005). *TIMSS 2007 assessment frameworks*. Chestnut Hill, MA: Boston College.

Olson, J. F., Martin, M. O., & Mullis, I. V. S. (2009). *TIMSS 2007 technical report*. Chestnut Hill, MA: Boston College.

Papanastasiou, E. (2002). Factors that differentiate mathematics students in Cyprus, Hong Kong, and the USA. *Educational Research and Evaluation*, *8*, 129–146.

Rautalin, M., & Alasuutari, P. (2007). The curse of success: The impact of OECD's Programme for International Student Assessment on the discourses of the teaching profession in Finland. *European Educational Research Journal*, *6*(4), 348–363.

Rupp, A. A., & Templin, J. L. (2008). Unique characteristics of diagnostic classification models: A comprehensive review of the current state-of-the-art. *Measurement*, *6*(4), 219–262.

Shepard, R. N. (1980). Multidimensional scaling, tree-fitting and clustering. *Science*, *210*, 390–398.

Shepard, R. N., & Arabie, P. (1979). Additive clustering: Representation of similarities as combinations of discrete overlapping properties. *Psychological Review*, *86*, 87–123.

Simola, H. (2005). The Finnish miracle of PISA: Historical and sociological remarks on teaching and teacher education. *Comparative Education*, *41*(4), 455–470.

Sireci, S. G., & Geisinger, K. F. (1992). Analyzing test content using cluster analysis and multidimensional scaling. A*pplied Psychological Measurement*, *16*(1), 17–31.

StataCorp. (2007). Stata statistical software: Release 10 [computer program]. College Station, TX: StataCorp LP.

Tatsuoka, K. K. (1983). Rule-space: An approach for dealing with misconceptions based on item response theory. *Journal of Educational Measurement*, *20*, 345–354.

Tatsuoka, K. K. (1985). A probabilistic model for diagnosing misconceptions in the pattern classification approach. *Journal of Educational Statistics*, *12*, 55–73.

Tatsuoka, K. K., Corter, J. E., & Tatsuoka, C. (2004). Patterns of diagnosed mathematical content and process skills in TIMSS-R across a sample of 20 countries. *American Educational Research Journal*, *41*(4), 901–926.

Um, E., Dogan, E., Im, S., Tatsuoka, K., & Corter, J. E. (2003, April). *Comparing Eighth Grade diagnostic test results for Korean, Czech, and American student*s. Paper presented at the Annual Meeting of the National Council on Measurement in Education, Chicago, IL.

von Davier, M. (2005). *A general diagnostic model applied to language testing data* (ETS Research Report RR-05-16). Princeton, NJ: ETS.

Wishart, D. (2005). Number of clusters. In B. S. Everitt & D. C. Howell (Eds.), *Encyclopedia of statistics in behavioral science* (pp. 1442–1446). Chichester, UK: Wiley.

TEDS-M: Diagnosing teacher knowledge by applying multidimensional item response theory and multiple-group models

Sigrid Blömeke
Humboldt University of Berlin, Berlin, Germany

Richard T. Houang
Michigan State University, Michigan, United States

Ute Suhl
Humboldt University of Berlin, Berlin, Germany

Researchers are still struggling to define a concept of pedagogical content knowledge that separates this dimension from content knowledge. Based on data from TEDS-M, an International Association of Educational Achievement (IEA) study of mathematics teacher education in 16 countries, this paper aims to contribute to this discourse by using different multidimensional approaches to modeling teacher knowledge. Another question of cross-cultural research is whether the characteristics of the latent traits examined and their interplay are homogeneous across countries (measurement invariance) or if it is necessary to treat the countries as separate groups. Our basic hypothesis is that more sophisticated multidimensional and multiple-group item response theory (IRT) models lead to valuable additional information that gives diagnostic insight into the composition of teacher knowledge. This is demonstrated using the TEDS-M data.

IERI Monograph Series: Issues and Methodologies in Large-Scale Assessments Volume 4

INTRODUCTION

The Teacher Education and Development Study in Mathematics (TEDS-M),[1] a multinational survey of mathematics teacher education in 16 countries, surveyed future primary and lower secondary teachers in their final year of teacher training. In addition to gathering data on the teacher trainees' backgrounds, the courses they were taking, and their beliefs about teaching, the study assessed the trainees' content knowledge and their pedagogical content knowledge, that is, the knowledge they would need to be successful in the classroom.[2] In this paper, we use the data from TEDS-M to examine different approaches to defining and subsequently scaling teacher knowledge. We also examine if such approaches are invariant across countries.[3]

DIMENSIONALITY OF TEACHER KNOWLEDGE

Latent traits such as reading literacy or mathematics literacy, typically found in the Progress in International Reading Literacy Study (PIRLS) or the Trends in Mathematics and Science Study (TIMSS), are relatively well defined. They serve different purposes and are usually applied in different contexts. Despite their measures having strong correlation, it is prudent to treat them as being conceptually different and therefore to scale them separately in unidimensional item response theory (IRT) models. This conceptual clarity does not exist with respect to teacher knowledge. Researchers are still struggling to define this latent trait and to identify its subdimensions (Graeber & Tirosh, 2008).

Teacher knowledge includes several cognitive abilities (Bromme, 1992; Shulman, 1985). Based on Shulman's initial work, two subject-related subdimensions of teacher knowledge can be distinguished:

- Content knowledge, which, in the case of TEDS-M as a study on mathematics teacher education, is *mathematics content knowledge* (MCK). MCK includes the fundamental definitions, concepts, and procedures of mathematics.

- Pedagogical content knowledge, which, in the case of TEDS-M, is *mathematics pedagogical content knowledge* (MPCK). This form of knowledge includes knowledge about how to present fundamental mathematical concepts to students, some of whom may have learning difficulties (for further details, see Tatto, Schwille, Senk, Ingvarson, Peck, & Rowley, 2008).

---

1 TEDS-M was funded by IEA, the US National Science Foundation (NSF; REC 0514431) and each participating country. In Germany, the study was funded by the German Research Foundation (DFG; BL 548/3-1). In the US, the study was funded by the GE Foundation, the Boeing Company, the Carnegie Corporation, and the Bill and Melinda Gates Foundation. Any views expressed in this paper are those of the authors and do not necessarily reflect the views of IEA or its funders.

2 For the first results from this study, see Blömeke, Kaiser, and Lehmann (2010a, 2010b), Blömeke, Suhl, and Kaiser (2011), and Tatto et al. (in press).

3 We thank Neelam Keer for her helpful comments on the final draft of this paper and the reviewers for their productive questions about the measurement models used, but we take responsibility for whatever errors we may have made.

Both subdimensions of teacher knowledge deal with mathematics but from different perspectives. Studies by Schilling, Blunk, and Hill (2007) and Krauss et al. (2008) demonstrate that while it is possible to distinguish between MCK and MPCK, the two are highly correlated. The challenge is to determine the appropriate model that defines the relationship between the two latent traits. One choice is between unidimensional and multidimensional IRT models.

Unidimensional models can stress the conceptual *overlap* of MCK and MPCK, in which case teacher knowledge is regarded as a single dimension and all items are scaled together. Or the model can stress the conceptual *difference* between MCK and MPCK, which means these two forms of knowledge are regarded as separate dimensions and the mathematics and the mathematics pedagogy items are scaled separately. This approach was used in TEDS-M. Figure 1 illustrates the two unidimensional models. It shows how the two types of items link to the respective latent variables.

Figure 1: Unidimensional approaches to scale MCK and MPCK (with respect to the notation, cf. Hartig & Höhler, 2008)

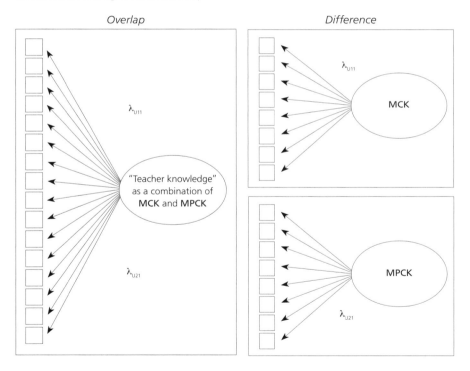

Multidimensional approaches, in contrast, can take the conceptual overlaps and differences into account at the same time. Multidimensional item response theory or MIRT (Reckase, 2009) is a relatively new but growing methodology for modeling the relationship of examinees to sets of test items as well as the relationship of the underlying latent traits when using the matrix of their responses (see, for example, Finkelman, Hooker, & Wang, 2010; Wang, Chen, & Cheng, 2004; Yao & Boughton, 2007). In the case of TEDS-M, two MIRT approaches are possible.

The first approach could be a two-dimensional scaling of MCK and MPCK, where each latent variable is treated as unidimensional ("between-item multidimensionality," Adams, Wilson, & Wang, 1997; "factorial simple," McDonald, 2000). MCK and MPCK items are restricted to load on one dimension. Their conceptual overlap is then expressed by a positive latent correlation of the two variables (see Figure 2).

The second approach could be a two-dimensional scaling of MCK and MPCK with a general and a nested factor ("within-item multidimensionality," Adams et al., 1997; "factorial complex," McDonald, 2000). This model would represent the idea that the nested factor MPCK is a mixture of different abilities and that mathematics pedagogy items measure this mix. According to this idea, solving mathematics pedagogy items requires not only MCK (as a general ability) but also specific MPCK (see Figure 3). In order to separate the latter from the former, the two latent variables are constrained to be uncorrelated.

Figure 2: Model of between-item multidimensionality

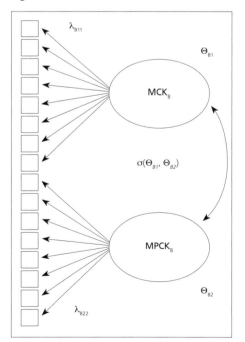

Figure 3: Model of within-item multidimensionality

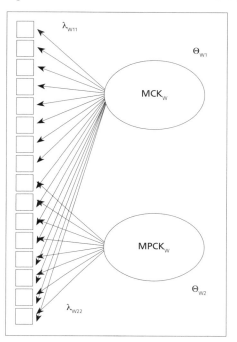

The different approaches to modeling the interplay of MCK and MPCK produce different scale scores, potentially leading to different interpretations. The within-item multidimensionality model depicted in Figure 3 allows for double loadings and therefore represents an elaborated model of the interaction between teachers and items. Hartig and Höhler (2008) demonstrated (with respect to the English literacy of German students) the value of such an approach, namely that it provides more information about the nested factor. Following their reasoning, we expect that it is only in such a *within model* that the strength of teachers on the nested factor (in the case of TEDS-M, MPCK) can be revealed for countries where mathematics pedagogy but not mathematics is stressed.

In contrast, in IRT models, where the two types of items are restricted to load only on one dimension, future teachers' achievement in MCK would obscure this strength. However, the advantage would be that we would essentially provide operational definitions of the two latent traits via the items themselves. In other words, we are relying on the face or content validity to provide meaning for the scaled scores. In this sense, the unidimensional model depicted on the right-hand side of Figure 1 and the between-item multidimensionality model depicted in Figure 2 are conceptually the same, except that all the items in the latter model are fitted together to yield a single statement of model fit.

In this paper, we examine the two latent traits, MCK and MPCK, and their relationships to the two types of items. We therefore restrict our attention to models where all the items are fitted simultaneously. This means that we examine the fit and the measurement properties of the two multidimensional approaches and of the unidimensional model with a single latent variable, "teacher knowledge" (see Figure 1 on the left-hand side). Because our focus is on contrasting the different models, the factor loadings of the items on their corresponding latent traits are constrained to be identical. This restriction simplifies the measurement models and limits the number of parameters to be fitted.

CULTURAL INVARIANCE

Another question we need to ask when modeling the subdimensions of teacher knowledge is whether the interplay of this dimension is homogeneous across countries (measurement invariance) or if we need to treat the countries as separate groups. A recurring controversy in the comparative education literature centers on whether one should try to establish a universal model of educational outcomes across countries or whether the differences among countries are of such importance that they should be modeled: see, for example, Heyneman and Loxley (1982) versus Comber and Keeves (1973) and the application of these two approaches to the TIMSS 2003 study by Ilie and Lietz (2010).

Consideration of this controversy with respect to our study meant that, irrespective of the scaling approach taken, we would need to model the participating TEDS-M countries as one homogeneous group or, more precisely, as multiple groups from the same population. In the first case (a universal model of educational outcomes across countries), we would need to treat model fit, loading patterns, variance explained, and latent correlations between MCK and MPCK as identical in all countries. The variances explained by the latent traits would then be the same in all countries. In the second case, we would need to allow cultural differences to manifest in differences in factor loadings, proportions of variance explained, and/or the latent correlations.

Moreover, even in the well-established field of studies on student achievement, the measurement quality is often slightly higher in English-speaking countries (Grisay, de Jong, Gebhardt, Berezner, & Halleux-Monseur, 2007; Schulz, 2009; Thorndike, 1973). An important reason for such non-equivalence is that, in a comparative study, most of the work associated with item development and item review is done in English. In addition, Grisay, Gonzalez, and Monseur (2009) suggest the following further potential sources for non-equivalence:

- Language problems, in that the mother tongue and the test language are not the same in some countries. This was the case, with respect to TEDS-M, in Botswana and the Philippines.

- Differences in educational traditions among Asian and Western countries or differences in the developmental state of participating countries. These may, in turn, appear (using our study to provide an example) as differences in teacher education curricula.

Although TEDS-M was a highly collaborative effort and although the field data were subject to many checks with respect to differential item functioning, differences might still exist in how well the models measure MCK and MPCK in different countries. This situation may manifest in how well the item variances are explained country by country.

RESEARCH QUESTIONS

To summarize, based on our assumption of teacher knowledge being multidimensional in nature, we expected that, across the TEDS-M countries, multidimensional models would be more likely than a unidimensional model to provide a better fit to the data. We anticipated the between and the within models depicted in Figures 2 and 3 would fit the data equally well, of course, because they are mathematically equivalent.[4] We also assumed that taking into account the multidimensional nature of teacher knowledge would be particularly favorable for the measurement of MPCK. Therefore, we expected that, across countries, the loadings of the mathematics pedagogy items on the underlying trait(s) would, in contrast to the loadings in the unidimensional model, vary and improve in the two-dimensional between and within models. We expected this pattern even though the loadings of the mathematics items on the underlying latent trait would be the same in all models.

In addition, and based on controversies and experiences from studies on student achievement, we expected that factor loadings, variances explained, and latent correlations between MCK and MPCK would differ from country to country. We expected to find that the countries where the test language did not match the language spoken at home would be set at a disadvantage when the future teachers worked on the items, and that the factor loadings, variances explained, and latent correlations would therefore be lower.

With respect to descriptive results, we expected that countries would show very different performance in MPCK as compared to their performance in MCK on the two-dimensional within model. The differences would vary according to the emphasis on mathematics pedagogical education in the teacher preparation programs of the respective countries. In particular, we expected the differences to be specifically apparent in countries such as Norway and the United States where mathematics

---

4 Note that this equivalence holds only if the factor loadings for each set of items (the mathematics and the mathematics pedagogy items, respectively) on their corresponding factors are constrained to be equal (see Rose, von Davier, & Xu, 2010, especially Appendix A; von Davier, Xu, & Carstensen, 2011). We discuss the equivalence mathematically in detail in Blömeke and Houang (2009; available on request from the authors). The *between model* conceptually corresponds to two simultaneously estimated Rasch models (one for each construct), thereby allowing for a correlation between the constructs. The *within model* is a reparameterization of the between model. Because the mathematics items have the same loadings whereas the mathematics pedagogy items have a different one for the latent variable MCK—and thus satisfy the two-parameter logistic definition of having multiple slopes—the *within model* is a simple case of the two-parameter logistic IRT model. Because the main aim of our paper is to demonstrate the implications—especially the potential value of the within modeling approach— of these different parameterizations for the interpretation of the TEDS-M data, we restricted ourselves to this kind of measurement model, which was also close to the scaling approach used by the TEDS-M International Study Center (see Tatto et al., in press).

pedagogy—but not mathematics—is stressed. For the two-dimensional between model, future teachers' achievement in MCK would obscure such differences.

DATA SOURCES

We used the international dataset from the TEDS-M assessment of future primary school teachers in their final year of teacher education for this paper. The total sample size was 13,400. The primary assessments consisted of five booklets with 104 items in total: 72 mathematics and 32 mathematics pedagogy items. Items were assigned to booklets following a balanced-incomplete-block design. The mathematics items covered the content areas "number" (as that part of arithmetic most relevant for primary teachers), "algebra," and "geometry," with each set of items having about equal weight, as well as a small number of items about "data" (as a hypernym for that part of probability and statistics most relevant for primary teachers). The mathematics pedagogy items included aspects of "curricular and planning knowledge" and "knowledge about how to enact mathematics in the classroom." These two sets of items were of about equal weight. The majority of items were complex multiple-choice items. Some of the items were partial-credit items.

Because primary school teachers are responsible for teaching multiple subjects, including mathematics, we examined in all TEDS-M countries, except Thailand,[5] a broad range of primary teacher education programs. Although 16 countries took part in the TEDS-M primary study, Canada was excluded because it did not meet the response rate requirements. Therefore, our sample consisted of 15 countries.

The sampling process for Norway was difficult, and the final country sample consisted of two subsamples that were likely to partly overlap. While information about the seriousness of this problem is not available, we realized that using only one subsample would lead to strongly biased country estimates. Combining both subsamples would lead to imprecise standard errors (for more details, see Tatto et al., in press). After an extensive research of the Norwegian literature about teacher education, combining TEDS-M data with publicly availably evaluation data from Norway (NOKUT, 2006), and recourse to expert reviews, we decided to combine the two subsamples in order to represent the future teachers' knowledge as appropriately as possible. However, the results should be regarded as a rough approximation only.

Finally, we used sampling weights in all the analyses so that all the countries were weighted equally. For each country, we adjusted the final sampling weights upwards or downwards so that the sum of weights for each country was equal to 500 cases.

---

5   In Thailand, the future teachers surveyed were primary mathematics specialists.

METHOD

We applied unidimensional and two-dimensional scaling models to the 104 items. We carried out calibration by applying, to the TEDS-M data, the IRT 2-parameter logistic model implemented in MPlus 5.2 (Muthén & Muthén, 2008), and using maximum likelihood estimation with robust standard errors (MLR). The estimation procedure took the multiple-groups and multiple-forms structure of the data into account (MLR is the MPlus default estimator when dealing with complex data structures). We used Samejima's (1969) graded-response model to model the partial credit items.

Because our focus was on comparing the different models, we constrained the factor loadings to be the same within each dimension. This constraint resulted in an identical estimate for the loadings of the same type of items, that is, mathematics versus mathematics pedagogy items, an outcome that facilitated comparison of the models.[6] Variances of the latent variables were fixed to 1. In the within-multidimensional model, the correlation between the two latent variables was restricted to 0. This meant that the specific MPCK factor was defined to be uncorrelated with the general MCK factor, which allowed us to use IRT as a "diagnostic aid" (Walker & Beretvas, 2003). Our evaluation of model fit was based on the log likelihood, which required us to take into account the number of parameters (adjusted Bayesian information criterion; see Schwartz, 1978).

When carrying out the multiple-group analyses, we used the mixture modeling procedure of MPlus, with countries as known classes. This procedure is the approach that Muthén and Muthén (2008) used when addressing this question. In the case of our study, it meant that all loading parameters and the correlation between MCK and MPCK (in the case of the between model) were estimated separately for each country.[7] For the single-group configuration, however, we restricted the parameters to be the same for all countries. Differences in the model fit between the multiple-group and the single-group configurations would point to differences among the countries.

After completing the calibration, we used the item-parameter estimates to estimate achievement for each respondent. We used, as individual-ability estimates, "expected a posteriori" (EAP), thereby assuming a standard normal distribution of the ability scores. In accordance with the practice in TEDS-M, we scored, when estimating scores for individuals, "not-reached" responses (which were scored as "missing" in the calibration) as "incorrect." Although Rose et al. (2010) demonstrated in a simulation study that this scoring procedure may result in bias, especially under the condition

---

6 As we pointed out in the previous footnote, this is not a standard 2PL IRT model, in the sense that slopes can vary across items. In contrast, the model, because of its restrictions, comes close to a 1PL (or Rasch) model. However, due to the double loadings of the mathematics pedagogy items or the different loadings of the mathematics items and the mathematics pedagogy items on the underlying MCK trait, respectively, we consider it is still justifiable to label the model as a (constrained) 2PL model.

7 In this sense, the procedure is actually the same as that used in the multiple-group IRT model (Bock & Zimowski, 1997). The only difference is its different labeling by Muthén and Muthén (2008), a situation that could cause confusion.

of a high proportion of not-reached responses, the proportion of such responses in the TEDS-M primary study was very small compared with the proportions in the simulation settings (MCK, 0.79%; MPCK, 1.14%). As a consequence, the correlations between the EAP estimates used in this paper and the EAP estimates obtained when scoring the not-reached items as missing were very high (single-factor model, 0.97; two-dimensional models, > 0.99). We standardized the EAP estimates (in logits) to a mean of 500 and a standard deviation of 100.

RESULTS

Measurement Properties of the Different Calibration Models

First, we examined the fit of the calibration models with data from all of the countries together (single-group configuration). The models contained 150 or 165 estimated parameters, respectively, for the unidimensional and two-dimensional models.[8] As expected, the two-dimensional between and within models showed a significantly better model fit than the unidimensional model (see Table 1, chi-squared difference test TRd = $x^2_{(15)}$ = 359.66, p < 0.0001). Both two-dimensional models produced the same log likelihood statistics because they were mathematically equivalent. This result supported our expectation of a multidimensional structure of teacher knowledge. The latent correlation between MCK and MPCK was high (0.85).

Table 1: Model fit for the different models under the single-group configuration

Model	Log likelihood	Scaling correction factor	Number of parameters	BIC$_{adj.}$	Latent correlation
One-dimensional model (teacher knowledge)	-365,822.06	2.11	150	732,592.88	—
Two-dimensional between model	-365,462.40	2.10	165	731,968.44	.85 (.02)
Two-dimensional within model	-365,462.40	2.10	165	731,968.44	.00 (.00)

Note: BIC$_{adj.}$ = adjusted Bayesian information criterion.

Second, we examined the loading patterns and the variance explained by the models in the single-group configuration. As we expected, the loadings of the mathematics items on the underlying MCK dimension were the same in all three models, whereas the loadings of the mathematics pedagogy items varied (see Table 2). The loadings of the mathematics pedagogy items on the underlying trait(s) were slightly higher in the two-dimensional models. But, more importantly, only the within model revealed the specific loading composition. Although the specific loadings of the mathematics pedagogy items on the MPCK trait were lower in the within model, they showed substantial additional loadings on MCK. All loadings were significant. This result points to the relevance of each dimension in this model.

---

8   That is, the item-difficulties or threshold parameters, factor loadings or item discrimination, class means, and, in the between-multidimensional model, the latent correlations.

Table 2: Standardized factor loadings and variance explained for the different models

Model	Factor loadings mathematics items	Factor loadings mathematics pedagogy items		R^2	
				MCK	MPCK
One-dimensional model (teacher knowledge)	.34 (.00)***	.28 (.01)***		.11 (.00)	.08 (.00)
Two-dimensional between model	.34 (.00)***	.30 (.01)***		.12 (.00)	.09 (.00)
Two-dimensional within model	.34 (.00)***	.25 (.00)*** MCK	.16 (.01)*** MPCK	.12 (.00)	.09 (.00)

Note: *** $p < .001$.

Note that the loading for the mathematics pedagogy items for the between model is a composite of the loadings of these items for the within model. Thus, the square of the value of 0.30 in the between model is the sum of the squares of 0.25 and 0.16 in the within model. In other words, as we pointed out above, the two models are mathematically equivalent.

The variance explained per item by the latent variables was higher for the mathematics items. This could be due to the smaller number of items and to a less well-defined MPCK trait, for which it is more difficult to construct items that measure it reliably.

Third, we examined if these results for the measurement properties of the calibration models applied to all countries (single-group configuration) or if there were differences among countries (multiple-group configuration). The comparison revealed a significantly better model fit of the two-dimensional multiple-group configuration (see Table 3, chi-squared difference test TRd = $x^2_{(42)}$ = 489.90, $p <$ 0.0001).

Table 3: Model fit of the two-dimensional between model under the single-group versus the multiple-group configuration

Model	Log likelihood	Scaling correction factor	Number of parameters	$BIC_{adj.}$
Single-group configuration	-365,462.40	2.10	165	731,968.44
Multiple-group configuration	-364,924.00	2.12	207	731,157.29

Notes:

$BIC_{adj.}$ = adjusted Bayesian information criterion.

The fit for the two-dimensional within model is identical to the fit of the between model documented here.

Table 4 shows the country variation in the measurement properties. The language use (match of test language versus language used at home) seemed to have a systematic relationship to how well the items were associated with the latent variables. The correlations at the country level between language use and factor loadings ranged from -0.44 to -0.74. In Botswana, Malaysia, and the Philippines, almost all future teachers spoke a language at home (mainly Setswana, Bahasa Melayu, or Filipino, respectively) that differed from the language they were tested in (English). In particular, the mathematics items showed smaller factor loadings for these three countries than for the other countries.

Language used at home seemed to have a stronger relationship to the mathematics items than to the mathematics pedagogy items, and this was evident in both the between model and the within model. This result is somewhat surprising given that—by nature—pedagogy could be regarded as more closely associated with verbal representations than with mathematics. That said, the latent correlations between MCK and MPCK were consistently high in all countries and uncorrelated to language use at home ($r = 0.06$).

As we again expected, the strength of the factor loadings and the amount of variance explained by the latent traits were significantly correlated with the developmental state of a country. We used the United Nations Human Development Index (HDI) as an indicator of the latter. However, the data revealed a relationship between measurement properties and country background for mathematics items but not for mathematics pedagogy items. The correlations between HDI and mathematics items were 0.36 and 0.26 for loadings and for variance explained, respectively, but the corresponding correlations ranged from only 0.06 to 0.14 for the mathematics pedagogy items.

Generally, the loadings of the mathematics items on the latent trait MCK were relatively high for the European countries. While regional differences between Asian and Western countries did not exist, the loadings were particularly high for the two Eastern Europe countries (Poland and Russia). They were 0.47 and 0.46, respectively. In contrast, the loadings for the other countries ranged from 0.19 to 0.39. The results were similar for the MPCK loading but not as pronounced.

Descriptive Summaries of Country Performance on MCK and MPCK

Table 5 shows the country descriptive summaries from the between and within models. Note that the two models produced identical scores for MCK; only one set is therefore included in the table. The country means for MPCK differed widely in the different models, however. In the between model, the rank order of countries according to MPCK was very similar to MCK, with all 15 countries having the same rank (nine countries), being within one or two ranks (five countries), or being within three ranks (one country) on the scales. Primary teachers from Taiwan and Singapore ranked 1 and 2 on both scales, respectively.

Table 4: Standardized factor loadings, variance explained, and latent correlations for the two-dimensional multiple-group models and parameter estimates correlations with HDI and language use

Country	HDI	Language use	Between model								Within model					
			MCK math items	SE	R²	MPCK math ped. items	SE	R²	Corr.	SE	MCK math items	SE	MCK math ped. items	SE	MPCK math ped. items	SE
Botswana	0.664	90.30	0.19	.03	0.04	0.22	.05	0.05	0.97	.20	0.19	.03	0.21	.07	0.04	.35
Chile	0.874	0.61	0.30	.01	0.09	0.32	.02	0.10	0.83	.05	0.30	.01	0.27	.02	0.18	.03
Georgia	0.763	3.25	0.37	.02	0.14	0.34	.03	0.11	0.65	.07	0.37	.02	0.22	.03	0.25	.03
Germany	0.940	2.20	0.39	.02	0.16	0.40	.02	0.16	0.83	.04	0.39	.02	0.33	.02	0.22	.02
Malaysia	0.823	87.18	0.21	.01	0.04	0.27	.02	0.07	0.85	.08	0.21	.01	0.23	.03	0.14	.04
Norway	0.968	1.59	0.37	.02	0.14	0.27	.02	0.07	0.92	.06	0.37	.02	0.25	.02	0.10	.04
Philippines	0.745	94.99	0.24	.02	0.06	0.20	.03	0.04	0.77	.15	0.24	.02	0.16	.03	0.13	.05
Poland	0.875	0.83	0.47	.01	0.22	0.44	.01	0.19	0.94	.02	0.47	.01	0.41	.01	0.15	.02
Russia	0.806	6.99	0.46	.01	0.22	0.38	.01	0.14	0.87	.03	0.46	.01	0.33	.01	0.19	.02
Singapore	0.918	42.80	0.34	.02	0.11	0.29	.02	0.08	0.75	.08	0.34	.02	0.21	.03	0.19	.03
Spain	0.949	13.85	0.27	.01	0.07	0.21	.01	0.05	0.90	.07	0.27	.01	0.19	.02	0.09	.04
Switzerland	0.955	6.14	0.33	.01	0.11	0.25	.02	0.06	0.77	.06	0.33	.01	0.19	.01	0.16	.02
Taiwan	0.932	29.59	0.38	.02	0.15	0.27	.02	0.07	0.95	.05	0.38	.02	0.25	.02	0.09	.04
Thailand	0.786	38.89	0.37	.01	0.14	0.26	.02	0.07	0.91	.05	0.37	.01	0.24	.02	0.11	.04
United States	0.950	1.78	0.34	.01	0.12	0.27	.02	0.07	0.88	.05	0.34	.01	0.23	.02	0.13	.03
Correlation* with HDI			**0.36**		0.26	0.13		0.11	0.06		**0.36**		0.14		0.11	
Correlation* with language use			-0.74		-0.68	-0.57		-0.53	0.07		-0.74		-0.49		-0.44	

Notes:

HDI: Human Development Index of the United Nations.

Language use at home: Proportion of future teachers with a mother tongue other than the test language (i.e., the official language of teacher education).

Between model: Mathematics items are loaded on MCK only, while mathematics pedagogy items are loaded on MPCK only.

Within model: Mathematics items are loaded on MCK only, while mathematics pedagogy items are loaded on both MCK and MPCK.

* These correlations were computed at the country level. Due to the small number of countries included and (in the case of language use) the extreme values, these are potentially subject to changes if the observations change.

Table 5: Means, standard errors, and standard deviations for the two-dimensional models

	MCK—between/within models				MPCK—between model				MPCK—within model		
	Mean	SE	SD		Mean	SE	SD		Mean	SE	SD
Taiwan	622	3.4	70	Taiwan	619	3.0	69	United States	544	2.3	97
Singapore	598	2.9	67	Singapore	601	3.0	66	Singapore	544	4.4	97
Switzerland	543	1.9	66	Switzerland	543	1.8	64	Norway	542	4.5	93
Russia	529	10.5	92	USA	529	3.8	71	Taiwan	520	2.8	87
Thailand	522	2.2	75	Norway	529	2.5	75	Malaysia	512	4.1	100
Norway	522	2.6	76	Russia	525	10.3	92	Switzerland	512	2.7	99
United States	522	4.1	72	Thailand	518	2.2	74	Spain	506	2.5	94
Germany	505	3.0	88	Germany	504	3.3	90	Philippines	499	7.4	95
Malaysia	485	2.2	58	Malaysia	488	2.6	61	Germany	494	4.3	107
Poland	480	2.1	102	Spain	478	2.8	61	Russia	489	8.0	102
Spain	476	2.9	61	Poland	477	2.0	103	Poland	484	2.7	98
Philippines	429	8.9	55	Philippines	432	9.5	55	Thailand	481	3.7	95
Botswana	428	6.4	53	Botswana	427	6.7	55	Chile	481	3.9	99
Chile	397	2.4	68	Chile	399	2.7	71	Botswana	477	11.1	94
Georgia	327	3.4	74	Georgia	326	3.3	73	Georgia	450	3.9	90

When we removed general mathematics ability from the latent trait MPCK, as was done in the within model, the picture changed. Only three countries now had the same rank according to MCK and MPCK, while the rank order for the other countries showed differences of up to six ranks. The result from the within model now showed future primary teachers from the United States with first place ranking in MPCK, tied with the future primary teachers from Singapore. Likewise, Norway, Malaysia, Spain, and the Philippines also ranked higher for their MPCK than for their MCK performance. In contrast, Russia and Thailand ended up below the international MPCK mean.

DISCUSSION

The two-dimensional between and within models provided significantly better fit estimates than the unidimensional model that assumed a single latent construct, "teacher knowledge." This result supports our contention that the nature of teacher knowledge is multidimensional. In accordance with Hartig and Höhler (2008), we can state that the between-multidimensional model describes the performance of future primary teachers on our mathematics and mathematics pedagogy items in a straightforward way. In contrast, the within model represents a more elaborated model of the interaction between teachers and items. Thus, the between model yields similar achievement information for MCK and MPCK, as revealed in the relative country ranks, whereas the within model yields distinctive profiles that are particularly evident in the case of MPCK.

Note that our summary relied on the kind of measurement models we used to define MCK and MPCK. Because our focus was on contrasting the different approaches to modeling multidimensionality and their implications for the interpretation of the TEDS-M results, we decided to keep the measurement models as simple as possible and as close to the scaling approach applied in TEDS-M as possible. It is most likely that a more complex measurement model, such as a two-parameter logistic IRT model without constraints on the factor loadings, would fit the data better or at least as well as our models, if only due to the larger number of free parameters. However, a more complex measurement model would not only make it more difficult to contrast the within and the between models, but also more difficult to interpret and thus obscure the parameterization benefits.

The main feature that, in our case, distinguishes the two two-dimensional models is that the within model attempts to isolate the specific MPCK trait from MCK. If we were to follow the descriptive results from the conditioned within model, they would suggest not only a special strength in mathematics pedagogy among the future primary teachers from the United States but also among those from Norway, Malaysia, Spain, and the Philippines. These countries moved visibly up in the rank order of countries from the within model. In contrast, with this model, future primary teachers from Taiwan and Singapore no longer outperformed the teachers from all the other countries, while the performance of teachers from Russia and Thailand moved below the international mean.

The relative importance of the within model as an appropriate representation of the strengths and weaknesses of the countries' respective mathematics teacher education provision becomes evident when we examine the correlation of MPCK with opportunities to learn (OTL) in teacher education. OTL were framed as content coverage in TEDS-M, specifically as "the content of what is being taught, the relative importance given to various aspects of mathematics and the student achievement relative to these priorities and content" (Travers & Westbury, 1989, p. 5, quoting Wilson). OTL were, in this sense, defined in terms of future primary teachers encountering occasions to learn about particular topics during their teacher education. Because subject-matter specificity is the defining element of an educational opportunity (Schmidt, McKnight, Valverde, Houang, & Wiley, 1997) and because TEDS-M is a study about "learning to teach mathematics," the particular topics reflected the areas of mathematics and mathematics pedagogy.

The correlation between the ipsative OTL[9] mean for mathematics pedagogy and the MPCK measure from the between model was almost zero ($r = -0.02$). But the correlation of the OTL mean with MPCK from the within model was $r = 0.30$. Thus, under the within model, the more a country had focused on mathematics pedagogy in relation to mathematics during primary teacher education, the more likely it would be to have a high MPCK mean.

The conclusions drawn from the results of the unconditioned-between versus the conditioned-within model would be different (see also Hartig & Höhler, 2008, with respect to English literacy). A potential explanation for this difference is the focus of primary teacher education. Coverage of mathematics content is highly relevant during teacher education in Taiwan, Singapore, Russia, and especially in Thailand, where, as we mentioned earlier, mathematics specialists are trained at the primary level. This focus is accurately expressed in these countries' MCK means.

In contrast, mathematics pedagogy is a very important focus of teacher education in Norway, Spain, and the United States, even at the cost of training in mathematics content. With the high conceptual and empirical overlap of MCK and MPCK (evident in the latent correlation), the low level of mathematics content knowledge superimposes on the relative strength in mathematics pedagogy. Its specialties are evident only in the within model that distinguishes between MCK influence on the solution of mathematics pedagogy items and specific MPCK influence. For those readers wanting to learn about MPCK in detail, the within model provides this diagnostic information.

---

9   In order to avoid cultural bias of self-reported data, which is a well-known problem in comparative studies (Triandis & Triandis, 1962; Van de Vijer & Leung, 1997), and which, in our case, would represent differences in the willingness to check a topic as studied or not studied in teacher education, relative (i.e., ipsative) measures were developed (see, for example, Cunningham, Cunningham, & Green, 1977; Fischer 2004):
  • (OTL_Number + OTL_Algebra + OTL_Geometry + OTL_Data) / 4 = OTL_Mathematics
  • (OTL_Foundations + OTL_Applications) / 2 = OTL_MathPedagogy
  • (OTL_Mathematics + OTL_MathPedagogy) / 2 = OTL_Subject
  • OTL_Mathematics_ipsative = OTL_Mathematics – OTL_Subject
  • OTL_MathPedagogy_ipsative = OTL_MathPedagogy – OTL_Subject.

With this conception, however, the MPCK results from the within model do not correspond to *test performance* on the mathematics pedagogy items, given that performance on mathematics pedagogy items is a function of both underlying traits. Performance requires a mix of mathematics and mathematics pedagogical abilities. Only the between model accurately reflects this reality. We therefore have to point out that both models have their uses and limitations and that it would not be appropriate to substitute one for the other.

Note that the latent correlation of 0.85 is high, which means that the multidimensionality observed is modest in size, even though it does appear to exist. An interesting follow-up research question in this context would cover the kind of relationship that exists between the conditioned MPCK and general pedagogical knowledge. Since extraction of MPCK is purposely uncorrelated with MCK, the former may be more strongly correlated to GPK for the within measure than for the between measure.

Evidence from our study also suggests that the MCK and MPCK assessments may not have been completely equivalent in all TEDS-M countries. Although rigorous quality control took place (as it always does in IEA studies), language and cultural differences might have been related to how well these traits were measured in the 15 countries. The differences by country complicate the development of a universal model of teacher knowledge.

To our surprise, the language problems seem to have been larger with respect to MCK than to MPCK. We attribute this result to a long history of schooling in the case of mathematics content knowledge. Its acquisition had probably already suffered from language disadvantages during primary and secondary school. In this sense, our study could raise the awareness of this problem.

A cultural influence on the measurement properties in TEDS-M may exist as well. The factor loadings were surprisingly high in the two Eastern European countries Poland and Russia. Although these countries were not specifically strongly involved in the test development, it seems that the two TEDS-M tests were more closely connected to mathematics and mathematics pedagogy traditions in these two countries. However, this conclusion can be only a very tentative one; the relationship needs to be examined in more detail.

What do these results on measurement invariance mean for the quality of the TEDS-M results? In reality, this question cannot be answered because it has to remain an open one. The number of countries in our study was only 15, with even smaller numbers of country groups from similar educational traditions (in order to determine a potential cultural bias) or with substantial proportions of teachers using a different language at home than they were tested in (in order to determine a potential language bias). In addition, there is no commonly agreed upon threshold above which a lack of measurement invariance would invalidate results from cross-country comparisons. Moreover, it would be naive to expect perfect test equivalence in comparative research.

Future research should examine in more detail the question of measurement invariance in TEDS-M. Hierarchical IRT and multiple-group confirmatory factor analysis provide the tools to determine important properties such as configural invariance, metric invariance, and scalar invariance (Fox, 2005; Vandenberg & Lance, 2000). Even if full invariance—which is rarely accomplished in cross-cultural research—cannot be determined in TEDS-M, such studies would reveal the extent to which partial invariance is supported. Approaches could then be taken to appropriately deal with such problems. Using hierarchical IRT, for example, de Jong, Steenkamp, and Fox (2007) were able to relax all invariance requirements across groups while retaining the possibility to make substantive comparisons. Such studies would be of relevance not only with respect to the TEDS-M assessment data but also, and perhaps more importantly, with respect to the OTL and beliefs data, given the likelihood of self-reported data being even more vulnerable to bias (Blömeke et al., 2010a, 2010b).

References

Adams, R., Wilson, M., & Wang, W. (1997). The multidimensional random coefficients multinomial logit model. *Applied Psychological Measurement, 21*, 1–23.

Blömeke, S., & Houang, R. T. (2009). *Comparing different scaling approaches in modeling teacher knowledge: The 6-country study "Mathematics Teaching in the 21st Century" (MT21).* Invited lecture at the University of Göteborg (Sweden), June 1, 2009.

Blömeke, S., Kaiser, G., & Lehmann, R. (Eds.). (2010a). *TEDS-M 2008: Professionelle Kompetenz und Lerngelegenheiten angehender Primarstufenlehrkräfte im internationalen Vergleich* [Cross-national comparison of the professional competency of and learning opportunities for future primary school teachers]. Münster, Germany: Waxmann.

Blömeke, S., Kaiser, G., & Lehmann, R. (Eds.). (2010b). *TEDS-M 2008: Professionelle Kompetenz und Lerngelegenheiten angehender Mathematiklehrkräfte für die Sekundarstufe I im internationalen Vergleich* [Cross-national comparison of the professional competency of and learning opportunities for future secondary school teachers of mathematics]. Münster, Germany: Waxmann.

Blömeke, S., Suhl, U., & Kaiser, G. (2011). Teacher education effectiveness: Quality and equity of future primary teachers' mathematics and mathematics pedagogical content knowledge. *Journal of Teacher Education, 62*(2), 154–171.

Bock, R. D., & Zimowski, M. F. (1997). Multiple-group IRT. In W. J. van der Linden & R. K. Hambleton (Eds.), *Handbook of modern item response theory* (pp. 433–448). New York, NY: Springer.

Bromme, R. (1992). *Der Lehrer als Experte: Zur Psychologie des professionellen Lehrerwissens* [The teacher as expert: On the psychology of teachers' professional knowledge]. Göttingen, Germany: Hans Huber.

Comber, L., & Keeves, J., (1973). *Science education in nineteen countries*. Stockholm, Sweden: Almqvist & Wiksell.

Cunningham, W., Cunningham, I., & Green, R. (1977). The ipsative process to reduce response set bias. *Public Opinion Quarterly, 41*, 379–384.

de Jong, M. G., Steenkamp, J.-B., & Fox, J.-P. (2007). Relaxing measurement invariance in cross-national consumer research using a hierarchical IRT model. *Journal of Consumer Research*, *34*, 260–278.

Finkelman, M., Hooker, G., & Wang, J. (2010). Prevalence and magnitude of paradoxical results in multidimensional item response theory. *Journal of Educational and Behavioral Statistics*, *35*, 744–761.

Fischer, R. (2004). Standardization to account for cross-cultural response bias: A classification of score adjustment procedures and review of research in *JCCP*. *Journal of Cross-Cultural Psychology*, *35*(3), 263–282.

Fox, J.-P. (2005). Multilevel IRT using dichotomous and polytomous items. *British Journal of Mathematical and Statistical Psychology*, *58*, 145–172.

Graeber, A., & Tirosh, D. (2008). Pedagogical content knowledge: Useful concept or elusive notion? In P. Sullivan & T. Woods (Eds.), *International handbook of mathematics teacher education: Vol. 1. Knowledge and beliefs in mathematics teaching and teaching development* (pp. 117–132). Rotterdam, the Netherlands: Sense Publishers.

Grisay, A., de Jong, J., Gebhardt, E., Berezner, A., & Halleux–Monseur, B. (2007). Translation equivalence across PISA countries. *Journal of Applied Measurement*, *8*(3), 249–266.

Grisay, A., Gonzalez, E., & Monseur, C. (2009). Equivalence of item difficulties across national versions of the PIRLS and PISA reading assessments. *IERI Monograph Series: Issues and Methodologies in Large-Scale Assessments*, *2*, 63–83.

Hartig, J., & Höhler, J. (2008). Representation of competencies in multidimensional IRT models with within-item and between-item multidimensionality. *Zeitschrift für Psychologie*, *216*(2), 89–101.

Heyneman, S., & Loxley, W. (1982). Influences on academic performance across high- and low-income countries: A re-analysis of IEA data. *Sociology of Education*, *55*, 13–21.

Ilie, S., & Lietz, P. (2010). School quality and student achievement in 21 European countries: The Heyneman-Loxley effect revisited. *IERI Monograph Series: Issues and Methodologies in Large-Scale Assessments*, *3*, 57–84.

Krauss, S., Brunner, M., Kunter, M., Baumert, J., Blum, W., Neubrand, M., & Jordan, A. (2008). Pedagogical content knowledge and content knowledge of secondary mathematics teachers. *Journal of Educational Psychology*, *100*(3), 716–725.

McDonald, R. (2000). A basis for multidimensional item response theory. *Applied Psychological Measurement*, *24*, 99–114.

Muthén, B., & Muthén, L. (2008). MPlus (Version 5.21) [Computer software]. Los Angeles, CA: Author.

NOKUT (Nasjonalt Organ for Kvalitet i Utdanningen). (2006). *Evaluering av Allmennlærerutdanningen i Norge 2006. Hovedrapport* [Evaluation of general teacher education in Norway: Main report]. Retrieved from http://evalueringsportalen.no/evaluering/evaluering-av-allmennlaererutdanningen-i-norge-2006.-del-l-hovedrapport

Reckase, M. (2009). *Multidimensional item response theory*. Dordrecht, Germany: Springer.

Rose, N., von Davier, M., & Xu, X. (2010). *Modeling non-ignorable missing data with IRT* (ETS Research Report No. 10–11), Princeton, NJ: ETS.

Samejima, F. (1969). Estimation of latent ability using a response pattern of graded scores. *Psychometrika Special Monograph Supplement, 17*.

Schilling, S., Blunk, M., & Hill, H. (2007). Test validation and the MKT measures: Generalizations and conclusions. *Measurement: Interdisciplinary Research and Perspectives, 5*(2–3), 118–127.

Schmidt, W., McKnight, C., Valverde, G., Houang, R., & Wiley, D. (1997). *Many visions, many aims: A cross-national investigation of curricular intentions in school mathematics.* Dordrecht, Germany: Kluwer.

Schulz, W. (2009). Questionnaire construct validation in the International Civic and Citizenship Education Study. *IERI Monograph Series: Issues and Methodologies in Large-Scale Assessments, 2*, 113–135.

Schwartz, G. (1978). Estimating the dimension of a model. *The Annals of Statistics, 6,* 461–464.

Shulman, L. (1985). Paradigms and research programs in the study of teaching: A contemporary perspective. In M. Wittrock (Ed.), *Handbook of research on teaching* (3rd ed., pp. 3–36). New York, NY: Macmillan.

Tatto, M., Schwille, J., Senk, S., Bankov, K., Rodriguez, M., Reckase, M., ... Peck, R. (in press). *The Mathematics Teacher Education and Development Study (TEDS-M): Policy, practice, and readiness to teach primary and secondary mathematics. International report.* Amsterdam, the Netherlands: International Association for the Evaluation of Educational Achievement.

Tatto, M., Schwille, J., Senk, S., Ingvarson, L., Peck, R., & Rowley, G. (2008). *Teacher Education and Development Study in Mathematics (TEDS-M): Policy, practice, and readiness to teach primary and secondary mathematics. Conceptual framework.* East Lansing, MI: College of Education, Michigan State University.

Thorndike, R. (1973). *Reading comprehension education in 15 countries: An empirical study.* Stockholm, Sweden: Almquist & Wiksell.

Travers, K., & Westbury, I. (1989). *The IEA study of mathematics I: Analysis of mathematics curricula* (Vol. 1). Oxford, UK: Pergamon Press.

Triandis, H. C., & Triandis, L. (1962). A crosscultural study of social distance. *Psychological Monographs: General and Applied, 76*, 1–21.

Vandenberg, R. J., & Lance, C. E. (2000). A review and synthesis of the measurement invariance literature: Suggestions, practices, and recommendations for organizational research. *Organizational Research Methods, 3*, 4–70.

Van de Vijver, F., & Leung, K. (1997). *Methods and data analysis for cross-cultural research.* Newbury Park, CA: Sage.

von Davier, M., Xu, X., & Carstensen, C. H. (2011). Measuring growth in a longitudinal large-scale assessment with a general latent variable model. *Psychometrika, 76*(2), 318–336. doi: 10.1007/S11336-011-9202-Z

Walker, C., & Beretvas, S. (2003). Comparing multidimensional and unidimensional proficiency classifications: Multidimensional IRT as a diagnostic aid. *Journal of Educational Measurement*, *40*(3), 255–275.

Wang, W., Chen, P., & Cheng, Y. (2004). Improving measurement precision of test batteries using multidimensional item response models. *Psychological Methods*, *9*, 116–136.

Yao, L., & Boughton, K. A. (2007). A multidimensional item response modeling approach for improving subscale proficiency estimation and classification. *Applied Psychological Measurement*, *31*(2), 83–105.

PISA test format assessment and the local independence assumption

Christian Monseur, Ariane Baye, Dominique Lafontaine, and Valérie Quittre
University of Liège, Liège, Belgium

Large-scale assessments of reading comprehension, notably OECD's Programme for International Student Achievement (PISA) and IEA's Progress in Reading Literacy Study (PIRLS), generally use paper-and-pencil tests in which a reading passage, with different questions based on it, is presented to the student. The PISA mathematics and science literacy tests also consist of a hierarchically embedded structure stimulus. In these surveys, cognitive data are scaled according to an item response theory (IRT) model. One of the cornerstones of standard IRT models is the assumption of local item independence (LII). Because multiple items are connected together to a common passage, items within a unit are not likely to be conditionally independent, which means that the independence assumption might be violated. In the first part of this study, Yen's Q_3 statistic was used to evaluate the importance of the local item dependency (LID) effect with respect to PISA 2000 and PISA 2003 data. The consequences of the violation of the LII assumption on the student performance distribution were then explored. Moderate but clear global context dependencies were detected in a large number of the PISA reading and mathematics units. Some reading and mathematics units showed additional significant pairwise local dependencies. Further, LID impacted on the variability of the student proficiencies, and the bias in the variability estimate strongly correlated with average country performance. Therefore, the consequence of LII violation in PISA is that the relative variability of low-performing countries is overestimated while the relative variability of high-performing countries is underestimated.

IERI Monograph Series: Issues and Methodologies in Large-Scale Assessments Volume 4
Copyright © 2011 by Educational Testing Service and International Association for the Evaluation of Educational Achievement.

INTRODUCTION

Large-scale assessments of reading literacy generally use paper-and-pencil tests in which a reading passage, with different questions (items) based on it, is presented to the student. This format seems to be the conventional reading test format for international assessments of reading conducted by the Organisation for Economic Co-operation and Development (OECD) and by the International Association for the Evaluation of Educational Achievement (IEA). The OECD has used this format for its PISA tests since 2000 (OECD, 2002). IEA used it for its first reading comprehension test in 1971 (Walker, 1976) and then continued to use it in its subsequent such tests (Elley, 1994; Mullis, Martin, Ruddock, O'Sullivan, Arora, & Erberer, 2007; Mullis et al., 2003).

This test format may be viewed as the most appropriate for assessing a complex process such as reading comprehension. In real-life situations, students have to use different cognitive processes to understand various components of the same text. Large-scale assessments are intended to evaluate whether some of these comprehension processes are successfully applied to a particular stimulus. For instance, the PISA reading literacy frameworks (OECD, 1999, 2009) describe the different components of reading literacy, and the reading test reflects these different dimensions. As summarized by Lee (2004), citing Mehrens and Lehman (1978) and Thissen, Steinberg, and Mooney (1989), "such a format makes it possible to measure examinees' understanding of the material from various perspectives and, at the same time, is cost-effective for both the item developers and examinees" (pp. 74–75).

OECD and IEA policies relating to international mathematics and science assessments differ with respect to test format. Since 2000, the PISA mathematics and science literacy tests have taken the form of a hierarchically embedded structure with several items related to a common stimulus. As discussed by Bao, Gotwals, and Mislevy (2006), one could argue that this hierarchical format may be desirable for mathematics and the sciences because it "reflect[s] real life situations in which sub-problems are interrelated and work is organized in steps" (p. 1). Because PISA aims to evaluate 15-year-olds' readiness for life, and proposes a non-curricular approach, the choice of test format is coherent with the general theoretical framework of the study (OECD, 2003, 2006). Conversely, IEA mathematics and science assessments include only one item per stimulus. This approach may be compared with the OECD one by contrasting the theoretical frameworks of the two surveys (grade- and curriculum-based for IEA). However, the IEA "one to one" approach in mathematics and science also presents a methodological advantage because it avoids passage-related local item dependence (LID), a phenomenon that can occur if groups of items are based on the same stimulus.

Since the IEA 1991 Reading Literacy Study (Elley, 1994; Wolf, 1995), cognitive data from international assessments have usually been scaled according to item response theory (IRT) models. One of the cornerstones of standard IRT models is the assumption of local item independence (LII). Because multiple items are connected together to a common passage, items within a unit are not likely to be conditionally independent, so the assumption might be violated. This conjectured lack of LII can have a substantial effect on the parameter estimates, on the standard error estimates, and on the fit of the IRT models (Balazs & De Boeck, 2006).

Our first purpose in conducting this study was to examine passage-related local item dependencies in PISA cognitive assessment materials. We used Yen's $Q3$ statistic for detecting LID (Yen, 1984), as well as the median and maximum $Q3$ values per unit. Our second purpose was to explore the impact of LII assumption violation on the student performance distribution in the context of PISA surveys. The question we asked ourselves here was this: Are these consequences of the LII assumption violation so large that alternative models should be investigated?

DEFINITION OF LOCAL ITEM DEPENDENCE

The standard unidimensional IRT model requires LII (Embretson & Reise, 2000; Lord & Novick, 1968). In such models, the probabilities that an examinee will provide a specific response to an item are a function of two components:

1. The test-taker's location on θ, that is, his or her ability; and

2. One or more parameters (difficulty parameter, discrimination parameter, and guessing parameter) describing the relationship of the item to θ.

For instance, according to the one-parameter Rasch model (Rasch, 1960), the probability that a person i will successfully answer an item j, given the person's ability, θ_i, and the item's difficulty, δ, is equal to:

$$P(X_{ij} = 1 \mid \theta_i, \delta_j) = \frac{\exp(\theta_i - \delta_j)}{1 + \exp(\theta_i - \delta_j)}$$

(1)

Because the likelihood of success depends only on the person's ability and on item characteristics, this means that the response to any item is unrelated to any other item given the latent trait θ. In other words, the unidimensionality assumption means that although the items may be highly intercorrelated in the test as a whole, this situation is a function that rests solely on the ability of the test-takers. When the trait level is controlled, local independence implies that no relationship remains between the items (Embretson & Reise, 2000).

If two items are locally independent, then success or failure on one item does not affect the probability of succeeding on the other item, given ability. Mathematically, if item j_1 and item j_2 are locally independent, then:

$$P(X_{ij1} = x_1 \text{ and } X_{ij2} = x_2 \mid \theta_i) = P(X_{ij1} = x_1 \mid \theta_i) \, P(X_{ij2} = x_2 \mid \theta_i)$$

(2)

where x_1 and x_2 are equal to 0 or 1. Given the trait level, θ, the conditional probability of achieving any pattern of scores on independent items is the product of the probabilities for the distinct items.

The violation of the LII assumption can have substantial consequences on test parameter estimates and on proficiency estimates. Research studies show that statistical analysis of data with LID is misleading (Chen & Thissen, 1997; Chen & Wang, 2007; Junker, 1991; Sireci, Thissen, & Wainer, 1991; Thissen, Steinberg, & Mooney, 1989; Tuerlinckx & De Boeck, 1998, 2001; Yen, 1993). Tuerlinckx and De Boeck (2001) mathematically and empirically demonstrated the impact of LID on difficulty and discrimination item parameters. They showed that if negative LID is not modeled, the discrimination parameters of the interdependent items are underestimated. They also showed that the discrimination parameter (α_j) depends on the difficulty of the item it interacts with, but not on the difficulty of the item itself. Due to its effect on the discrimination parameter, the negative LID deflates the item information (as a function of the square of α_j), and the standard error of measurement is underestimated. It is therefore essential to ensure the accuracy of the discrimination parameters, given that they index the item quality and therefore the test quality (Chen & Wang, 2007). LID can also strongly bias the variance estimate of student ability (Junker, 1991) and produce biased proficiency estimates.

Yen (1993) identified several potential causes of LID. Some of them are independent of the item's content: external assistance (e.g., assistance from a teacher), fatigue (stimuli tend to be more difficult when they appear at the end of a test), practice, item or response format, speediness (if test-takers do not reach item j, they will surely not reach item $j+1$), and so on. Chen and Thissen (1997) call this last type of local dependency "surface local dependence."

Other causes of LID cited by Yen (1993) relate to the content of items, namely, item chaining (items organized in steps) and explanation arising out of previous answer and stimulus dependence. This stimulus-LID can be produced by an examinee's unusual level of interest in or background knowledge about the common stimuli or by the fact that information used to answer different items is interrelated in the stimulus. Chen and Thissen (1997) define this category of dependence as "underlying local dependence" because it assumes a separate trait common to each set of locally dependent items. These separate traits can therefore be regarded as minor dimensions existing beside the unique essential latent dimension θ.

DETECTION OF LOCAL ITEM DEPENDENCE

Recent years have seen increased interest in the development of methods for detecting and/or modeling LID. Chen and Thissen (1997) reflected on four potential statistics as detection indices of local dependence for pairs of items: (a) the X^2 statistic, (b) the G^2 statistic, (c) the standardized Φ coefficient difference, and (iv) the standardized log-odds ratio difference. These four statistics are commonly used to examine covariation of two-way contingency tables, which here are the expected[1] and the observed contingency tables.

Although the standardized Φ coefficient difference and the standardized log-odds ratio difference have the advantage of having signs that correspond to the direction of the association, they have the great drawback of being undefined when zero is observed in some of the cells of the contingency tables. Chen and Thissen (1997) chose the Pearson's X^2 statistic and the likelihood ratio G^2 statistic and compared them with another statistic proposed by Yen (1984), the Q_3, which is a pairwise index of correlation of the residuals from the IRT model. They showed that X^2 and G^2 indices appear somewhat less powerful than Yen's Q_3 statistic for "underlying local dependence" stemming from the contents of items, but equally powerful for "surface local dependence" operating between non-reached items at the end of a test.

Conditional-covariance-based statistical tools developed in order to estimate characteristics of a multidimensional latent space (DETECT) can also be used for detecting the type of LID that we focus on in this study (Stout, 2000; Stout, Habing, Douglas, Kim, Roussos, & Zhang, 1996). This method, which is based, like the Q_3 statistic, on the null covariance for all item pairs with respect to the latent trait level, can be used to reveal homogeneous item subsets that represent a separate dimension (Balazs & De Boeck, 2006).

Because our study investigated passage-related LIDs, which can be considered the focus of the underlying local dependence model, we chose Yen's Q_3 for our analyses. The advantage of this statistic is that it allowed us to investigate the association after the θ latent trait had been partially removed.

The Q_3 is based on the residuals' Pearson product moment correlations. The principle of the analysis is to take into account the test-taker's abilities. As mentioned earlier, in IRT models the probability of success depends on the test-taker's ability and on item properties such as difficulty and other parameters. Inter-item correlations are therefore expected and observed. However, for any particular level of difficulty, inter-item correlations should be equal to 0 (conditional independence assumption). Analyzing the residuals provides a way of controlling for student proficiency. This is because the residuals are the differences between the individuals' observed scores and their respective predicted scores. If some sets of items present a significant level of residual correlation, then those items can be considered as locally dependent (Yen, 1993).

---

1   Predicted by the IRT model.

Yen's Q_3 statistic requires analysts to first compute the item parameter estimates and the student proficiency estimates (maximum likelihood estimate). These estimates are then used to compute the student's expected performance on each item.

The expected performance of student i for item j with $k+1$ consecutive integer-possible scores (i.e., from 0 to k) is equal to:

$$E_{ij} = \sum_{k=1}^{k} kp(X_{ij} = k | \theta_i)$$ (3)

In the case of the dichotomous Rasch model, in which k can take only two values, that is, 0 and 1, the expected score is equal to:

$$E_{ij} = p(X_{ij} = 1 | \theta_i, \delta_j) = \frac{\exp(\theta_i - \delta_j)}{1 + \exp(\theta_i - \delta_j)}$$ (4)

The residual is the deviation between the student's observed performance (raw score) and the expected item performance, that is:

$$R_{ij} = X_{ij} - E_{ij}$$ (5)

The Q_3 statistic is the correlation between residuals of two items across students and therefore reflects LID between the two items. This statistic thus reflects only linear dependencies between residuals. "It should be noted, however, that local independence is a broader assumption than zero correlations; local independence also includes nonlinear or higher-order relationship between the items" (Embretson & Reise, 2000, p. 188).

Because the item score is included in both raw scores and theta-predicted scores, the Q_3 value tends to be slightly negatively biased. As Yen (1993) demonstrated, when LII is true, the Q_3 value is approximately $\frac{-1}{(n-1)}$, where n is the total number of items.

Chen and Wang (2007) distinguished negative and positive correlations between dependent items. They confirmed by simulation that negative interactions would lead to clearly negative Q_3 (in contrast to the slightly negative Q_3 exhibited by independent pairs of items), whereas positive dependencies would, logically, lead to positive Q_3. They also showed that an identical degree of dependence between two items can produce different absolute Q_3 values. They therefore questioned the appropriateness of setting a cut point (e.g., ± 0.2) for detecting item interaction.

Chen and Wang (2007) accordingly proposed that simulation should be used for the computation of the sampling variance of the Q_3 statistic. Each computed Q_3 value (and particularly those Q_3 values where LID is suspected) is compared to the corresponding distribution of Q_3 statistics obtained from a number of simulated datasets, assuming LII, and modeled according to the same specifications (identical IRT model, identical item, and person parameter estimates). A pair of items will be definitively recognized as interrelated if the Q_3 statistic computed on the real dataset falls outside the critical range of the corresponding empirical distribution of "zero LID" Q_3 values.

MODELING LOCAL ITEM DEPENDENCE

The development of methods for modeling item dependencies parallel the development of procedures designed to detect item dependence. In line with Hoskens and De Boeck (1997) and Wilson and Adams (1995), we distinguish three main approaches.

The first approach involves methods that consider the independence requirement between subsets of items rather than between isolated items. Wainer and Kiely (1987) label these subsets of items, when analyzed together, as "testlets." In this category of methods, testlet scoring replaces item scoring, that is, the scores within a testlet are summed and each score usually represents a category of a polytomous item. This approach is applied in the graded response model (Samejima, 1969), the dispersion-location model (Andrich, 1985), the partial credit model (Wright & Masters, 1982), and the rating scale model (Andrich, 1978). Wang, Cheng, and Wilson (2005, p. 7) cite Warner (1995), who considered that the partial credit model is a "suitable model if the test contains a minor proportion of dependent items." Yan (1997), employing the partial credit model at the unit level, showed that context-dependent items present better-fitting statistics at the unit level than at the item level. However, this approach circumvents the LID phenomenon rather than modeling it, with the disadvantage that information at the item level is lost.

The second approach, usually denoted the fixed-effects approach (Chen & Wang, 2007; Haberman, 2007; Smits, De Boeck, & Verhelst, 2003; Wang & Wilson, 2005b), models the LID into the IRT models. The response patterns of a testlet are modeled by including additional fixed item interaction parameters beside the parameters of individual items. The total item information is therefore preserved while the LII assumption can be dropped. Because the interaction parameter is constant on the logit scale, LID is viewed as an item characteristic and the unidimensionality assumption still holds.

In the third approach (random-effects models), interaction parameters introduced into the standard item response models are variable, that is, dependent on the test-taker's ability. LID is thus viewed as a personal characteristic. The resulting model is therefore multidimensional because new dimensions are added to capture the dependencies. Among a large number of these random-effects models, we can cite the Bayesian random-effects model for testlets (Bradlow, Wainer, & Wang, 1999; Wang, Bradlow, & Wainer, 2002), the random weights linear logistic test model (LLTM) (Rijmen & DeBoeck, 2002), the random-effects two-facet model (Wang & Wilson, 2005a), the Rasch subdimension model (Brandt, 2008), and the two-tier full-information item-factor analysis model (Cai, 2010; Rijmen, 2009).

METHOD

The OECD's Programme for International Student Achievement (PISA) is a survey of the reading, mathematics, and science proficiencies of 15-year-olds still enrolled in school. PISA is an ongoing data collection program, with students assessed every three years. For each data collection, one of these three domains is deemed the major one. It represents about two-thirds of the cognitive testing material. The first PISA data collection occurred in 2000, with reading as the major domain; the second occurred in 2003, with mathematics as the major domain.

In PISA, the main survey items are allocated to clusters (13 in PISA 2003), each one of which is designed to represent 30 minutes of testing. Clusters do not mix items from different domains (i.e., reading literacy, mathematics literacy, and science literacy). Clusters are then assembled in several test booklets (9 in PISA 2000, 13 in subsequent data-collection cycles), with each booklet composed of four clusters. Each student participating in the international assessment is randomly assigned one of the test booklets. The two-hour test is divided into two sessions separated by a short break. Because the provision of a trend indicator of student performance constitutes one of the major purposes of PISA, items from previous cycles are included in subsequent assessments for equating purposes.

The analyses that we report in this study were performed on reading data from PISA 2000[2] and mathematics data from PISA 2003. We excluded from our analyses data for non-OECD countries. As shown in Table 1, most of the PISA reading items are clustered in units that contain an average of 3.5 items. In mathematics, there are more single than clustered items; the average number of items per unit is 1.6.

Table 1: Number of units and items by major domain and cycle

Cycle	Domain	Number of units including several items	Number of units including a single item	Number of items	Average number of items per unit
2000	Reading	34	3	129	3.5
2003	Mathematics	19	34	84	1.6

We began our analyses by examining, through computation of the Q_3 statistic, stimulus-related local-item dependencies in the PISA databases. We gave separate consideration to two general types of dependence:

1. A global context local dependence that Hoskens and De Boeck (1997) call "combination dependency." This form of LID can occur when the issue treated in the stimulus influences the response on each item within the unit.

2. A specific pairwise local dependence that occurs when two (or maybe more) items are embedded or if the information required for answering two items is linked in the stimulus. In this case, a residual correlation would only be observed between this pair of items.

---

2 Turkey and the Slovak Republic did not participate in PISA 2000.

We then explored the impact of a violation of the LID assumption on the student performance distribution (particularly for reading in PISA 2000 and for mathematics in PISA 2003). As we will explain, we included any sources of LID in these analyses.

The first of our two purposes required the following steps: (a) calibration of the item parameters, (b) generation of the student proficiency point estimates, (c) computation of the residuals, and (d) computation of the Q_3 statistic. However, some transformations of the data were necessary before we implemented these four steps. First, we had to exclude from the databases the students with special needs in education, who took a shorter test (UH booklet). Second, in order to control for LID due to speediness, we recoded the non-reached items as non-administered items.

Non-reached items were represented as consecutive missing-by-design values clustered at the end of the test session except for the first item in the series of items not responded to, which was retained as an omitted response. Usually in international surveys such as PISA, the responses to non-reached items are considered as missing by design. They are therefore not included in the item calibration, and are seen as incorrect with respect to computation of student performance estimates (for more details, see Adams & Wu, 2002; OECD, 2005).

The way PISA treats non-reached items means that artificial local item dependencies can be produced.[3] Chen and Thissen (1997) identify these as "surface local dependence." As we mentioned earlier, a test-taker not reaching item j will also not reach item $j+1$. This situation therefore generates a correlation between residuals. Table 2 illustrates the difference in average inter-item residual correlation within four reading units of PISA 2000, when the non-reached items were included or not included. These results illustrate that non-reached items artificially generate correlations between residuals.

Table 2: Average residual correlations[a] for four PISA 2000 reading units computed without and with non-reached items as valid answers

Unit	Average residual correlations[a]		
	Mean percentage of non-reached items	Without non-reached items (missing answer)	With non-reached items (wrong answer)
R076	9.08	0.08	0.17
R067	4.74	0.12	0.27
R219	0.45	0.24	0.23
R227	0.28	0.02	0.03

Note: [a] The mean residuals correlation is computed per OECD country. It is the mean of the pairwise correlations within the unit. The results are averaged across countries.

---

3   For alternative ways of dealing with non-reached items, see Rose, von Davier, and Xu (2010) and Yamamoto and Everson (1997).

Because the first aim of our study was to investigate LID due to the hierarchical structure of the test only, we had to exclude non-reached items from the statistical analyses. This approach ensures that detected LIDs are not a result of the speediness of the test-taker. However, because the second part of our study involved exploration of the consequences of violating the LID assumption on the student performance distribution, we considered non-reached items as incorrectly answered.

After recoding and transformation, we scaled the data with the IRT partial credit model described by Wright and Masters (1982). This model is an extension of the Rasch model for polytomous items (which are scored as correct, partially correct, or incorrect). We used ConQuest software (Wu, Adams, Wilson, & Haldane, 2007) to carry out the item calibration, and we estimated the item parameters on the international calibration samples, which consisted of simple random samples of 500 students per OECD country.[4] Point estimates of students' abilities (maximum likelihood estimates) were then computed on the whole sample. Item parameter estimates and student proficiency point estimates were computed without weighting the data.

Finally, we computed, for each country, residual item correlations for each pair of items within a unit on weighted data, and obtained a Q_3 matrix for each unit (for one k-item unit, there are $\frac{k}{(k-1)/2}$ Q_3 values of the matrix). Following Yen (1993), we used two key values to analyze the effect: the median and maximum values within the unit's Q_3 matrix. The results are summarized as an average across OECD countries.

The median Q_3 value is an indicator of the dependence at the unit level. It reveals the global context dependence due to use of a common passage for multiple items. As we have already mentioned, the common passage structure of a test can also engender LID, once one particular pair of items is correlated in the unit. This type of stimulus-related LID would be revealed if the maximum Q_3 value of the matrix were significantly higher than its corresponding median Q_3 value.

The second aim of our study was to evaluate the consequences of LID on countries' estimates. (If the LII assumption is violated, the mean and the standard deviation of student performance may be biased.) To explore this effect of LID, we computed student proficiency estimates at the item level as well as at the unit (testlet) level. At the unit level, we recoded the cognitive data for reading in PISA 2000 and for mathematics in PISA 2003 in order to form testlets. We then summed the scores within a testlet, with each score representing a category of a polytomous item, and scaled the PISA cognitive data according to the one-parameter partial credit model.

Before forming the testlets, we needed to recode some data to ensure the validity of the comparison between the scaling at the unit level and the scaling at the item level. If an item was deleted for a country, the whole unit for that country was deleted. These data transformations ensured that the two raw scores—one for the unit scaling

---

4 We carried out the item calibration on a subsample of 500 students by country in order to follow the PISA procedure and to ensure that each country equally contributed to the calibration

and one for the item scaling—were identical for each student. The data of students attending a special education school and who answered a shorter test were then deleted.

As previously described, we scaled the data for these second analyses with the IRT partial credit model (Wright & Masters, 1982), and used ConQuest software (Wu et al., 2007) to implement item and unit calibration. We estimated item parameters on the same international calibration samples as those selected for the item dependence measurement and then computed estimates of students' abilities (maximum likelihood estimates). Our final step was to transform the students' proficiency estimates (from both scalings) on the new scale with an OECD mean of 500 and an OECD standard deviation of 100. Each OECD country contributed equally to the computation of the two linear transformations.

RESULTS AND DISCUSSION

Detection of LID

Table 3 shows that 32 of the 34 PISA reading-related units had positive values on the median Q_3 statistic. However, this statistic should have been slightly negative if LII within the units had held true. PISA 2000 reading passages thus generate global context dependencies, but their magnitudes seem fairly moderate: all but one of the units had, on average for the OECD countries, a median Q_3 value of less than 0.10.

Although the global context dependencies appear to be quite limited in the reading units, we can observe substantial Q_3 values for some pairs of residuals within no fewer than five units. The maximum Q_3 values[5] given in Table 3 were, on average for OECD countries, greater than 0.20 for R219, R216, R083, R227, and R040. These five reading units included at least one pair of items that are interrelated in the stimulus.

The released unit R040 (Figure 1) illustrates this type of LID. The stimulus consists of one short text and two graphs, with five items relating to these. Question 2 and Question 3 show correlated residuals, with an average maximum Q_3 value across the OECD countries of 0.21. A close examination of the content of this unit reveals the embedded structure of these two items. Obviously, if students cannot specify in which period the graph starts (Question 2), they will probably not be able to infer the reason why this start point (Question 3) has been chosen, and vice versa. Thus, the first item provides clues to the answer to the second one, explaining the positive LID detected.

Table 4 shows that the median Q_3 values were largely high in the PISA 2003 mathematics materials. Six units presented average median Q_3 statistics that were clearly positive, that is, greater than or equal to 0.10. Note that in the mathematics units consisting of pairs of items, the median and maximum Q_3 values were the same. The results showed that unit M406, with three items, was the only unit that gave an apparent global context LID (as measured by the median Q_3 value). However, because this unit has not been released, we cannot provide an illustration of it here.

---

5 For one k-item unit, the maximum Q_3 value is the maximum residual correlation out of the $\frac{k}{(k-1)/2}$ values of the Q_3 matrix.

Table 3: Summary statistics for local dependence in reading, PISA 2000

Unit	Number of items	Median Q_3		Max Q_3	
		OECD average	SD	OECD average	SD
R219	3	0.13	0.05	0.33	0.11
R067	3	0.09	0.04	0.14	0.06
R246	2	0.08	0.05	0.08	0.05
R076	3	0.07	0.04	0.13	0.04
R220	5	0.07	0.04	0.19	0.05
R216	5	0.06	0.04	0.25	0.08
R238	2	0.06	0.03	0.06	0.03
R086	3	0.05	0.03	0.10	0.04
R091	3	0.05	0.04	0.08	0.04
R237	2	0.05	0.04	0.05	0.04
R101	6	0.04	0.04	0.13	0.09
R100	4	0.04	0.03	0.09	0.03
R061	4	0.03	0.03	0.14	0.05
R239	2	0.03	0.05	0.03	0.05
R081	4	0.03	0.03	0.14	0.06
R083	5	0.03	0.02	0.31	0.09
R055	4	0.02	0.02	0.09	0.04
R110	4	0.02	0.02	0.12	0.05
R122	2	0.02	0.04	0.02	0.04
R070	4	0.02	0.02	0.12	0.04
R234	2	0.02	0.04	0.02	0.04
R225	3	0.02	0.03	0.06	0.04
R119	7	0.02	0.02	0.14	0.05
R236	2	0.01	0.07	0.01	0.07
R040	5	0.01	0.03	0.21	0.06
R228	3	0.01	0.03	0.04	0.05
R088	5	0.01	0.03	0.09	0.07
R102	5	0.01	0.01	0.10	0.04
R104	4	0.01	0.03	0.15	0.06
R120	4	0.01	0.03	0.05	0.03
R111	4	0.01	0.03	0.08	0.07
R227	5	0.00	0.02	0.25	0.08
R077	5	-0.01	0.03	0.08	0.08
R245	2	-0.02	0.08	-0.02	0.08

Figure 1: PIRLS test Unit R040, Lake Chad

Figure 1 shows changing levels of Lake Chad, in Saharan North Africa. Lake Chad disappeared completely in about 20,000 BC, during the last Ice Age. In about 11,000 BC it reappeared. Today, its level is about the same as AD 1000.

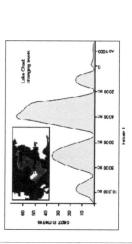

Figure 1

Figure 2 shows Saharan rock art (ancient drawings or paintings found on the walls of caves) and changing patterns of wildlife.

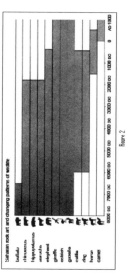

Figure 2

Use the information about Lake Chad in the opposite page to answer the questions below.

Question 1: LAKE CHAD   R040Q02

What is the depth of Lake Chad today?

A   About two metres.
B   About fifteen metres.
C   About fifty metres.
D   It has disappeared completely.
E   The information is not provided.

Question 2: LAKE CHAD   R040Q03A-0 1 9

In about which year does the graph in Figure 1 start?

Question 3: LAKE CHAD   R040Q03B-0 1 5

Why has the author chosen to start the graph at this point?

Question 4: LAKE CHAD   R040Q04

Figure 2 is based on the assumption that?

A   the animals in the rock art were present in the area at the time they were drawn.
B   the artists who drew the animals were highly skilled.
C   the artists who drew the animals were able to travel widely.
D   there was no attempt to domesticate the animals which were depicted in the rock art.

Question 5: LAKE CHAD   R040Q06

For this question you need to draw together information from Figure 1 and Figure 2.

The disappearance of the rhinoceros, hippopotamus and aurochs from Saharan rock art happened?

A   at the beginning of the most recent Ice Age.
B   in the middle of the period when Lake Chad was at its highest level.
C   after the level of Lake Chad had been falling for over a thousand years.
D   at the beginning of an uninterrupted dry period.

143

Table 4: Summary statistics for local dependence in mathematics, PISA 2003

Unit	Number of items	Median Q_3		Max Q_3	
		OECD average	SD	OECD average	SD
M124	2	0.25	0.07	0.25	0.07
M406	3	0.24	0.07	0.36	0.06
M496	2	0.22	0.05	0.22	0.05
M402	2	0.20	0.07	0.20	0.07
M413	3	0.11	0.04	0.30	0.08
M828	3	0.10	0.03	0.19	0.05
M144	4	0.09	0.03	0.17	0.05
M704	2	0.08	0.04	0.08	0.04
M603	2	0.05	0.04	0.05	0.04
M438	2	0.04	0.07	0.04	0.07
M302	3	0.03	0.02	0.08	0.04
M810	3	0.02	0.02	0.16	0.05
M155	4	0.02	0.02	0.08	0.04
M564	2	0.02	0.03	0.02	0.03
M446	2	0.01	0.03	0.01	0.03
M150	3	0.00	0.02	0.03	0.03
M421	3	-0.01	0.02	0.03	0.04
M411	2	-0.02	0.04	-0.02	0.04
M520	3	-0.03	0.03	0.07	0.04

The qualitative analysis of the released units M124 and M402 illustrated pairwise item dependence. The reason for the high dependence between the two items composing Unit M124 seems quite apparent: for both items, students are required to replace one of the elements of the formula given in the stimulus with a number given in the stem. The only difference between the two items presented in Figure 2 is that, in Question 1, it is the numerator that needs to be replaced; in Question 3, it is the denominator. Question 3 is more difficult than Question 1 because a final transformation has to be made to convert steps per minute into meters per minute. Given that both items require the ability to (a) replace a symbol in the same formula with a figure, and (b) solve a simple equation, it is not surprising that a high dependence between the two items is observed.

Unit M402, Internet Relay Chat (Figure 3), produced a similar type of dependence. This unit of two items had a Q_3 value (median and/or maximum) of 0.20. Both items in the unit required students to compute the time lag between Berlin and Sydney. Although this time lag is visually presented in the stimulus, students had to determine its value (nine hours) and its direction (Sydney later than Berlin). The first item required a simple use of this time lag, whereas the second item, which is more difficult,[6] required students to first use the time lag and then compare time ranges. The communality of the tasks measured in the two items might explain the detected dependence.

Figure 2: PISA assessment Unit M124, Walking

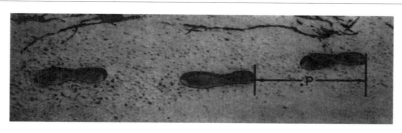

The picture shows the footprints of a man walking. The pacelength P is the distance between the rear of two consecutive footprints.

For men, the formula, $\frac{n}{P}$ =140, gives an approximate relationship between n and P where,

n = number of steps per minute, and

P = pacelength in metres

WALKING QUESTION 1

The formula applies to Heiko's walking and Heiko takes 70 steps per minute. What is Heiko's pacelength?

WALKING QUESTION 3

Bernard knows his pacelength is 0.80 metres. The formula applies to Bernard's walking. Calculate Bernard's walking speed in metres per minute and in kilometres per hour.

Our analysis of the remaining mathematics units with high LID did not help us further isolate the source of the dependence. The similarities in the cognitive processes required for answering items might be one potential source of dependence. The contexts of the mathematics stimuli might be another potential source.

It would be inappropriate to make a strict comparison between the sources of dependence in reading and in mathematics, given that reading units have, on average, 3.5 items while mathematics units have 1.6. However, the results make it possible to hypothesize that PISA mathematics stimuli are more likely than PISA reading passages to generate dependence.

Our analyses showed LID in the PISA 2000 and 2003 materials. For the majority of the units, we detected a slight global context dependence, and for some units significant pairwise item interaction. These results confirm the hypothesis that passages can generate undesirable local interactions. They also corroborate Lee's results (2004), showing local dependence among items within passages in a test of English as a foreign language. Lee investigated the LID within passages and within item types by computing Q_3 statistics on both real and simulated (LII assumed) datasets. The author observed positive values for the average within-passage Q_3 (ranging from .02 to .08 across 10 passages), whereas the same values for the simulated data were all negative. Lee concluded that there was moderate but clear evidence of positive passage-related LID supplemented by some item pairs with extreme Q_3 values (.20).

6   OECD item parameters were 0.204 for the first item and 1.119 for the second one.

Figure 3: Presentation of PIRLS assessment Unit M402, Internet Relay Chat

INTERNET RELAY CHAT

Mark (from Sydney, Australia) and Hans (from Berlin, Germany) often communicate with each other using "chat" on the internet. They have to log on to the internet at the same time to be able to chat.

To find time to chat, Mark looked up a chart of world times and found the following:

Greenwich 12 Midnight   Berlin 1 AM   Sydney 10:00 AM

INTERNET RELAY CHAT Question 1

At 7.00 PM in Sydney, what time is it in Berlin?

INTERNET RELAY CHAT Question 2

Mark and Hans are not able to chat between 9.00 AM and 4.30 PM their local time, as they have to go to school. ALso, from 11.00 PM till 7.30 AM their local time they won't be able to chat because they will be sleeping.

When would be a good time for Mark and Hans to chat? Write the local times in the table.

Place	Time
Sydney	
Berlin	

The results furthermore support, to some extent, the analyses that Cai (2010) performed on a subset of PISA 2000 data (Booklet 8) using a random effect model, corroborating the residual dependence between items within units.

Effect on Countries' Estimates

The foregoing analyses identified undesirable dependence in some reading and mathematics units. As the standard deviations of the Q_3 statistics in Table 3 show, LID varied across countries. For instance, Q_3 for Unit M124 ranged from 0.13 to 0.40.

In order to test whether there was a relationship between the extent of LID and country performance, we computed the average of median and maximum Q_3 statistics per country and then correlated these with the country performance estimates.

In reading, the low-achieving countries showed, on average, a higher LID than did countries with higher student scores (a correlation of -0.33 with median Q_3). We also observed a higher correlation in mathematics (a correlation of -0.60 with median Q_3). Because the LID varied according to the country performance level, it was essential that we analyzed the impact of such LID on country proficiency mean and standard deviation estimates.

For each student who participated in PISA 2000, we computed two new maximum likelihood estimates: one from the scaling at the item level, and one from the scaling at the testlet level. As described earlier, we considered non-reached items for these analyses as incorrect answers when conducting the item calibration and computing the proficiency estimates.

In the following paragraphs we describe the influence of the LID on country performance mean and standard deviation estimates for reading and then for mathematics. Table 5 presents the country mean and standard deviation estimates, as well as their respective differences for the two scores (i.e., the *unit* score and the *item* score).

The shift in the country mean estimates ranged from -1.4 to 1.7 points on the PISA reading scale, and the shift in the country standard deviation ranged from -3.4 to 4.3. The change in the country mean estimates could be regarded as negligible, given that the range represents only 0.03 of an OECD standard deviation. However, Schafer and Graham (2002) consider a bias as not negligible if it is higher than half a standard error. If we apply this rule, the difference in Korea, New Zealand, and Mexico is higher than half a standard error on the mean estimate.[7] The change in the standard deviation estimates is more of an issue, as the range is substantially higher (about eight points on the PISA scale) than half a standard error of the standard deviation estimates in more than half of the OECD countries. Furthermore, the change in the standard deviation closely correlates (-0.97) with the country proficiency mean estimates, as shown in Figure 4.

The *x*-axis of Figure 4 shows the country mean estimates based on the scaling at the item level. A positive value on the *y*-axis means that the standard deviation from the item scaling is higher than the standard deviation from the unit scaling. In other words, the unit scaling increases the standard deviation estimates for high-performing countries and decreases them for low-performing countries. A comparison between the OECD's top-performing country and the OECD's bottom-performing country illustrates the shift in the standard deviation. With the item scaling, the two countries present similar standard deviations (89.4 and 88.7 for Finland and Mexico respectively). These figures are quite different with respect to the unit scaling (92.8 for Finland and 84.4 for Mexico).

Unfortunately, this analysis does not disentangle the influence of LID on the country performance indicators from that of non-reached items. Because non-reached items increased LID and because the percentage of non-reached items correlated with the country performance, the relationship represented in Figure 4 might mainly be an artifact of non-reached items.

---

7   Note that we estimated standard errors according to the PISA sampling design. More precisely, we estimated them using a variant of the balanced repeated replication, that is, Fay's methodology (Fay, 1989; see also Judkins, 1990; Rust & Rao, 1996).

Table 5: Mean and standard deviation estimates[a] on the combined reading scale per type of scaling

Unit	Mean		SD		Differences	
	Item scaling	Unit scaling	Item scaling	Unit scaling	Means	Standard deviation
Mexico	424.8	426.0	88.7	84.4	-1.29	4.30
Luxembourg	444.0	444.9	106.9	103.1	-0.95	3.80
Portugal	469.6	469.8	98.9	96.7	-0.21	2.17
Greece	473.6	473.5	98.3	96.6	0.13	1.69
Poland	477.4	477.4	101.9	100.0	0.05	1.98
Italy	487.1	486.5	92.1	91.6	0.59	0.53
Hungary	487.5	487.0	92.5	91.3	0.52	1.20
Germany	491.4	491.6	101.6	101.0	-0.17	0.54
Switzerland	491.5	491.8	103.1	102.1	-0.38	0.99
Spain	492.0	491.1	87.2	85.7	0.97	1.47
Denmark	494.3	494.0	100.9	100.5	0.29	0.48
Czech Republic	497.8	497.0	89.0	88.9	0.88	0.12
United States	501.1	501.7	105.3	105.6	-0.56	-0.26
Norway	502.1	502.3	105.0	105.1	-0.25	-0.08
France	502.2	501.6	94.8	94.5	0.56	0.31
Island	503.4	503.0	94.5	94.3	0.32	0.18
Austria	505.3	504.6	92.7	92.5	0.65	0.15
Belgium	509.1	509.5	104.9	105.1	-0.36	-0.19
Sweden	512.8	512.7	94.5	95.3	0.12	-0.78
Japan	518.6	517.7	89.8	90.4	0.88	-0.61
United Kingdom	519.7	520.4	102.6	104.9	-0.74	-2.33
Korea	520.1	518.4	73.7	75.0	1.74	-1.29
Ireland	523.3	523.4	95.0	96.8	-0.08	-1.81
Australia	524.6	525.4	101.8	104.3	-0.82	-2.45
New Zealand	525.2	526.6	108.6	111.3	-1.41	-2.68
Netherlands	527.7	527.4	89.4	91.4	0.28	-1.94
Canada	530.5	530.9	95.5	98.2	-0.36	-2.73
Finland	543.2	543.6	89.4	92.8	-0.39	-3.41

Note: [a] Computed across students.

To overcome this limitation, we re-conducted these analyses after deleting any student with at least one non-reached item in reading. The correlation between the country mean estimates and the change in the country standard deviation estimates was not affected. The observed correlation therefore did not result from the non-reached item issue.

Figure 4: PISA 2000 country proficiency mean estimates (at the item level) and changes in the standard deviation estimates for reading

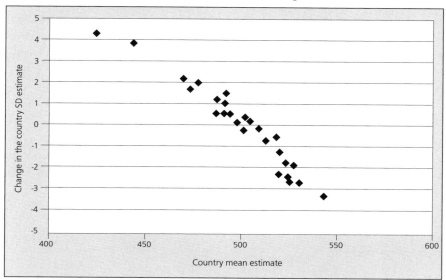

In mathematics, over 40 percent of the 2003 items were not embedded within a unit made up of several items (as shown in Table 1 in the previous section). Our analyses of the impact of LID were therefore performed on the whole set of items and also on the units with several items only. Table 6 presents the minimum and maximum shifts for the mean estimates and for the standard deviation estimates.

Not surprisingly, the ranges of the shifts were considerably larger for the analyses that we conducted on units with several items only. Furthermore, the correlation between the shift in the standard deviation and the country performance was equal to -0.60 for the whole set of items, but it was equal to -0.91 when we included only units with several items in the computation of student proficiency estimates. This correlation of -0.91 upholds the results observed in reading, namely, LID alters the standard deviation, and the shift in the standard deviation closely correlates with the country performance. Nevertheless, these results need to be confirmed by application of other IRT models such as a generalized partial credit model.

Table 6: Shifts in the mean and standard deviation estimates,[a] PISA 2003 mathematics

		Minimum	Maximum
Whole set of items	Mean	-0.43	0.31
	SD	-1.03	0.67
Units with several items only	Mean	-1.38	0.55
	SD	-1.81	2.19

Note: [a] On average for OECD countries.

CONCLUSION

Since the IEA 1991 Reading Literacy Study (Elley, 1994; Wolf, 1995), cognitive data from international assessments have usually been scaled according to IRT models. One of the assumptions of IRT models is local item independence (LII). PISA assessment material, as well as that of other international assessments of reading literacy such as PIRLS, is hierarchically structured, which means that several items relate to a single context. This embedded structure may violate the assumption of LII. As Embretson and Reise (2000) state, "Practically, local independence is violated when item responses are linked" (p. 188).

Our research was aimed at detecting local item dependence (LID) in PISA and measuring its impact on student performance distribution. We used the PISA 2000 and the PISA 2003 cognitive data for this exercise. Two types of passage-related LID were distinguished. The first was the global context dependence that can occur when the issue treated in the stimulus influences the response to each item that composes the unit. The second was the specific pairwise local dependence that occurs when two items are embedded or if the information required for answering both items is linked in the stimulus.

Using Yen's Q_3 statistic, we detected moderate but clear global context dependencies in a large number of the units in both reading and mathematics. Several reading and mathematics units also showed substantial LID, mainly due to the manifestation of specific pairwise local dependencies. However, mathematics passages seemed to engender higher LID than reading texts.

We furthermore found LID impacts on some important PISA indicators. Passage- and context-related LID, in combination with a test-taker speed effect observed in 2000 test data, influenced the variability of the student proficiencies. The range of the shifts in the standard deviation of proficiency estimates can reach about 10 points on the PISA scales. This represents 0.10 of the international standard deviation. In addition, as highlighted in this study, the bias in the variability estimate strongly correlates with the average country performance. The relative variability of low-performing countries is thus overestimated, while the relative variability of high-performing countries is underestimated.

In summary, the main conclusions of the research are (a) moderate LID due to the use of common passages in reading units but substantial LID due to a speed effect, (b) LID in several mathematics units, and (c) a bias in the performance variability that closely correlates with country performance.

The moderate global context dependencies in PISA reading and mathematics units support Lee's (2004) analysis of student performance data from an English as a foreign language reading comprehension test. Our results also agree with the "testlet effects" that Cai (2010) detected when modeling a subset of mathematics and reading PISA 2000 data (Booklet 8), using a random effect approach.

The dependence identified in several mathematics units could result from similarities in the cognitive processes involved in several items or from the specificity of the context. In this particular domain, prior knowledge about the stimulus or the interrelation of the information required to answer different items are certainly major sources of LID.

In addition to the slight general LID due to a common text, we found several reading passages marked by a rather high pairwise item dependence that could result, as in mathematics, from interrelated response indications. In PISA, these cases of pairwise dependence are quite limited because test developers carefully construct units to avoid such dependencies. Nevertheless, LID detection could be useful in the pre-test step for flagging item pairs exhibiting extreme LID. That, in turn, would achieve a better understanding of its sources.

As a number of authors have already reported (see, for example, Junker, 1991; Scott & Ip, 2002), LID can bias the variance estimate of student ability. Our research has shown a strong relationship between the bias in the standard deviation due to LID and country performance. This link certainly contributes to the well-known interactions between the measurement instrument and the countries.

The results of this research highlight the importance of LID analyses on the field trial data. The cost/benefit ratio of clustered items needs to be discussed, as correlated items conditional on student proficiency generate a loss of information. A mathematics unit of the kind shown in Figure 2 perfectly illustrates the inefficiency of correlated items that are conditional on the latent trait. The results also emphasize the importance of interpreting survey indicators in their methodological contexts, and they provide a reminder of the relative character of such indicators. After all, a change in the standard deviation will automatically affect percentages of students in the lowest and highest proficiency levels. Furthermore, because the variability of student proficiencies is one of the indicators used to evaluate the equity of education systems, a country can appear more or less equitable depending on the scaling model.

Our study has several limitations, however. First, we consider it would be worthwhile, as a confirmatory activity, to check the presence of LID due to reading passages in other international surveys such as IEA's Progress in International Reading Literacy Study (PIRLS) (Foy & Kennedy, 2008). Preliminary analyses performed on PIRLS 2006 data seem to show similar findings (Quittre & Monseur, 2010). Nevertheless, the apparently slight degree of LID in the PISA reading material is somewhat counterintuitive and therefore deserves cross-validation. In addition, it would be useful to construct the sampling distribution of the Q_3 statistic using simulation of the type proposed by Chen and Wang (2007). This approach would enable the significance level of the LID coefficients to be computed. Finally, we advocate not only extending these analyses to non-OECD countries, which usually have lower achievement levels than OECD countries, but also further investigating potential interactions between LID and certain country or student characteristics.

References

Adams, R., & Wu, M. (2002). *PISA 2000 technical report*. Paris, France: Organisation for Economic Co-operation and Development.

Andrich, D. (1978). A rating formulation for ordered response categories. *Psychometrika*, *43*, 561–573.

Andrich, D. (1985). A latent trait model for items with response dependencies: Implications for test construction and analysis. In S. E. Embretson (Ed.), *Test design: Developments in psychology and psychometrics* (pp. 245–275). New York, NY: Academic Press.

Balazs, K., & De Boeck, P. (2006). *Detecting local item dependence stemming from minor dimensions: Interuniversity Attraction Pole statistics network* [technical report]. Retrieved from http://www.stat.ucl.ac.be/IAP

Bao, H., Gotwals, A. W., & Mislevy, R. J. (2006). *Assessing local item dependence in building explanation tasks* (PADI Technical Report 14). Menlo Park, CA: SRI International.

Bradlow, E. T., Wainer, H., & Wang, X. (1999). A Bayesian random effects model for testlets. *Psychometrika*, *64*, 153–168.

Brandt, S. (2008). Estimation of a Rasch model including subdimensions. In M. von Davier & D. Hastedt (Eds.), *IERI monograph series: Issues and methodologies in large-scale assessments* (Vol. 1, pp. 51–70). Princeton, NJ: IEA-ETS Research Institute.

Cai, L. (2010). A two-tier full-information item factor analysis model with applications. *Psychometrika*, *75*, 581–612.

Chen, C. T., & Wang, W. C. (2007). Effects of ignoring item interaction on item parameter estimation and detection of interacting items. *Applied Psychological Measurement*, *31*, 388–410.

Chen, W. H., & Thissen, D. (1997). Local dependence index for item pairs using item response theory. *Journal of Educational and Behavioral Statistics*, *22*, 265–289.

Elley, W. B. (1994). The IEA study of reading literacy: Achievement and instruction in thirty-two school systems. Oxford, UK: Pergamon Press.

Embretson, S. E., & Reise, S. P. (2000). *Item response theory for psychologists*. Mahwah, NJ: Lawrence Erlbaum Associates.

Fay, R. E. (1989). Theory and application of replicate weighting for variance calculations. *Proceedings of the Survey Research Methods Section, ASA*, 212–217.

Foy, P., & Kennedy, A. M. (2008). *PIRLS 2006 user guide for the international database*. Chestnut Hill, MA: Boston College.

Haberman, S. J. (2007). The interaction model. In M. von Davier & C. H. Carstensen (Eds.), *Multivariate and mixture distribution Rasch models* (pp. 201–216). New York, NY: Springer.

Hoskens, M., & De Boeck, P. (1997). A parametric model for local dependencies among test items. *Psychological Methods*, *2*, 261–277.

Judkins, D. (1990). Fay's method for variance estimation. *Journal of Official Statistics*, *6*(3), 223–239.

Junker, B. W. (1991). Essential independence and likelihood-based ability estimation for polytomous items. *Psychometrika*, *56*, 255–278.

Lee, Y.-W. (2004). Examining passage-related local item dependence (LID) and measurement construct using Q_3 statistics in an EFL reading comprehension test. *Language Testing*, *21*, 74–100.

Lord, F. M., & Novick, M. (1968). *Statistical theories of mental test scores*. Reading, MA: Addison-Wesley.

Mullis, I. V. S., Martin, M. O., Ruddock, G. J., O'Sullivan, C. Y., Arora, A., & Erberber, E. (2007). *TIMSS 2007 assessment frameworks*. Chestnut Hill, MA: Boston College.

Mullis, I. V. S., Martin, M. O., Smith, T. A., Garden, R. A., Gregory, K. D., Gonzalez, E. J., ... O'Connor, K. M. (2003). *TIMSS assessment frameworks and specifications 2003* (2nd ed.). Chestnut Hill, MA: Boston College.

Organisation for Economic Co-operation and Development (OECD). (1999). *Measuring student knowledge and skills: A new framework for assessment*. Paris, France: Author.

Organisation for Economic Co-operation and Development (OECD). (2002). *PISA 2000 technical report*. Paris, France: Author.

Organisation for Economic Co-operation and Development (OECD). (2003). *The PISA 2003 assessment framework*. Paris, France: Author.

Organisation for Economic Co-operation and Development (OECD). (2005). *PISA 2003 technical report*. Paris, France: Author.

Organisation for Economic Co-operation and Development (OECD). (2006). *Assessing scientific, reading and mathematical literacy: A framework for PISA 2006*. Paris, France: Author.

Organisation for Economic Co-operation and Development (OECD). (2009). *PISA 2009 assessment framework*. Paris, France: Author.

Quittre, V., & Monseur, C. (2010, July). *Exploring local item dependency for items clustered around common reading passage in PIRLS data*. Paper presented at the fourth IEA International Research Conference, Gothenburg, Sweden. Retrieved from http://www.iea-irc.org

Rasch, G. (1960). *Probabilistic models for some intelligence and attainment tests*. Copenhagen, Denmark: Danish Institute for Educational Research.

Rijmen, F. (2009, July). *A hierarchical factor IRT model for items that are clustered at multiple levels*. Paper presented at the 74th Annual Meeting of the Psychometric Society, Cambridge, England.

Rijmen, F., & De Boeck, P. (2002). The random weights linear logistic test model. *Applied Psychological Measurement*, *26*, 271–285.

Rose, N., von Davier, M., & Xu, X. (2010). *Modeling non-ignorable missing data with IRT* (ETS Research Report No. RR-10-10). Princeton, NJ: ETS.

Rust, K. F., & Rao, J. N. K. (1996). Variance estimation for complex surveys using replication techniques. *Survey Methods in Medical Research*, *5*, 283–310.

Samejima, F. (1969). Estimation of latent ability using a response pattern of graded scores. *Psychometrika Monograph Supplement*, *17*, 1–100.

Schafer, J. L., & Graham, J. W. (2002). Missing data: Our view of the state of the art. *Psychological Methods*, *7*, 147–177.

Scott, S. L., & Ip, E. H. (2002). Empirical Bayes and item clustering effects in a latent variable hierarchical model: A case study from the National Assessment of Educational Progress. *Journal of the American Statistical Association*, *97*, 409–419.

Sireci, S. G., Thissen, D., & Wainer, H. (1991). On the reliability of testlet-based tests. *Journal of Educational Measurement*, *28*, 237–247.

Smits, D. J. M., De Boeck, P., & Verhelst, N. (2003). Estimation of the MIRID: A program and a SAS-based approach. *Behavior Research Methods, Instruments, & Computers*, *35*, 537–549.

Stout, W. (2002). Psychometrics: From practice to theory and back. *Psychometrika*, *67*, 485–518.

Stout, W., Habing, B., Douglas, J., Kim, H. R., Roussos, L., & Zhang, J. (1996). Conditional covariance-based nonparametric multidimensionality assessment. *Applied Psychological Measurement*, *20*, 331–354.

Thissen, D., Steinberg, L., & Mooney, J. A. (1989). Trace lines for testlets: A use of multiple-categorical-response models. *Journal of Educational Measurement*, *26*, 247–260.

Tuerlinckx, F., & De Boeck, P. (1998). Modeling local item dependencies in item response theory. *Psychologica Belgica*, *38*, 61–82.

Tuerlinckx, F., & De Boeck, P. (2001). The effect of ignoring item interactions on the estimated discrimination parameters in item response theory. *Psychological Methods*, *6*, 181–195.

Wainer, H., & Kiely, G. L. (1987). Item clusters and computerized adaptive testing: A case for testlets. *Journal of Educational Measurement*, *24*, 185–201.

Walker, D. (1976). *The IEA Six Subject Survey: An empirical study of education in twenty-one countries*. Stockholm, Sweden: Almqvist & Wiksell.

Wang, X., Bradlow, E. T., & Wainer, H. (2002). A general Bayesian model for testlets: Theory and applications. *Applied Psychological Measurement*, *29*, 109–128.

Wang, W.-C., Cheng, Y.-Y., & Wilson, M. R. (2005). Local item dependence for items across tests connected by common stimuli. *Educational and Psychological Measurement*, *65*, 5–27.

Wang, W.-C., & Wilson, M. R. (2005a). The Rasch testlet model. *Applied Psychological Measurement*, *29*, 126–149.

Wang, W.-C., & Wilson, M. R. (2005b). Exploring local item dependence using a random-effects facet model. *Applied Psychological Measurement*, *29*, 296–318.

Wilson, M., & Adams, R. J. (1995). Rasch models for item bundles. *Psychometrika*, *60*, 181–198.

Wolf, R. M. (1995). The IEA Reading Literacy Study: Technical report. The Hague, the Netherlands: International Association for the Evaluation of Educational Achievement (IEA).

Wright, B. D., & Masters, G. N. (1982). Rating scale analysis. Chicago, IL: MESA Press.

Wu, M. L., Adams, R. J., Wilson, M. R., & Haldane, S. A. (2007). ACER ConQuest version 2.0: Generalised item response modelling software [computer program]. Camberwell, Victoria, Australia: ACER Press.

Yamamoto, K., & Everson, H. (1997). Modeling the effects of test length and test time on parameter estimation using the HYBRID model. In J. Rost & R. Langeheine (Eds.), Applications of latent trait and latent class models in the social sciences (pp. 89–98). New York, NY: Waxman.

Yan, J. (1997, March). Examining local item dependence effects in a large-scale science assessment by a Rasch partial credit model. Paper presented at the Annual Meeting of the American Educational Research Association, Chicago, IL.

Yen, W. M. (1984). Effects of local item dependence on the fit and equation performance of the three-parameter logistic model. Applied Psychological Measurement, 2, 125–145.

Yen, W. M. (1993). Scaling performance assessments: Strategies for managing local item dependence. Journal of Educational Measurement, 30, 187–213.

INFORMATION FOR CONTRIBUTORS

Content

IERI Monograph Series: Issues and Methodologies in Large-Scale Assessments is a joint publication between the International Association for the Evaluation of Educational Achievement (IEA) and Educational Testing Service (ETS). The goal of the publication is to contribute to the science of large-scale assessments so that the best available information is provided to policy-makers and researchers from around the world. Papers accepted for this publication are those that focus on improving the science of large-scale assessments and that make use of data collected by programs such as IEA-TIMSS, IEA-PIRLS, IEA-Civics, IEA-SITES, U.S.-NAEP, OECD-PISA, OECD-PIAAC, IALS, ALL, etc.

If you have questions or concerns about whether your paper adheres to the purpose of the series, please contact us at IERInstitute@iea-dpc.de.

Style

The style guide for all IERI publications is the *Publication Manual of the American Psychological Association* (5th ed., 2001). Manuscripts should be typed on letter or A4 format, upper and lower case, double spaced in its entirety, with one-inch margins on all sides. The type size should be 12 point. Subheads should be at reasonable intervals to break the monotony of lengthy text. Pages should be numbered consecutively at the bottom of the page, beginning with the page after the title page. Mathematical symbols and Greek letters should be clearly marked to indicate italics, boldface, superscript, and subscript.

Please submit all manuscripts electronically, preferably in MS-Word format and with figures and tables in editable form (e.g., Word, Excel). It is particulary important that figures and tables are clear and of a quality that aids editing and reproducibility. Please send your submission to the editorial team at IERInstitute@iea-dpc.de and attach the Manuscript Submission Form, which can be obtained from the IERI website: www.ierinstitute.org. For specific questions or inquiries, send emails to editors at the same address. Only electronic submissions are accepted.

Author Identification

The complete title of the article and the name of the author(s) should be typed only on the submission form to ensure anonymity in the review process. The pages of the paper should have no author names, but may carry a short title at the top. Information in the text or references that would identify the author should be deleted from the manuscript (e.g., text citations of "my previous work," especially when accompanied by a self-citation; a preponderance of the author's own work in the reference list). These may be reinserted in the final draft. The author (whether first-named or co-author) who will be handling the correspondence with the editor and working with the publications people should submit complete contact information, including a full mailing address, telephone number, and email addresses.

Review Process

Papers will be acknowledged by the managing editor upon receipt. After a preliminary internal editorial review by IERI staff, articles will be sent to two external reviewers who have expertise in the subject of the manuscript. The review process takes anywhere from three to six months. You should expect to hear from the editor within that time regarding the status of your manuscript. IERI uses a blind review system, which means the identity of the authors is not revealed to the reviewers. In order to be published as part of the monograph series, the work will undergo and receive favorable technical, substantive, and editorial review.

Originality of Manuscript and Copyright

Manuscripts are accepted for consideration with the understanding that they are original material and are not under consideration for publication elsewhere.

To protect the works of authors and the institute, we copyright all of our publications. Rights and permissions regarding the uses of IERI-copyrighted materials are handled by the IERI executive board. Authors who wish to use material, such as figures or tables, for which they do not own the copyright must obtain written permission from IERI and submit it to IERI with their manuscripts.

Comments and Grievances

The Publications Committee welcomes comments and suggestions from authors. Please send these to the committee at IERInstitute@iea-dpc.de.

The right-of-reply policy encourages comments on articles recently published in an IERI publication. Such comments are subject to editorial review and decision. If the comment is accepted for publication, the editor will inform the author of the original article. If the author submits a reply to the comment, the reply is also subject to editorial review and decision.

If you think that your manuscript is not reviewed in a careful or timely manner and in accordance with standard practices, please call the matter to the attention of the institute's executive board.

Publication Schedule

There is one publication per year. This publication will consist of five to seven research papers. Manuscripts will be reviewed and processed as soon as they are received and will be published in the next available monograph series. In the event that, in a single year, there are more than seven accepted manuscripts, the editorial committee determines whether the manuscript(s) will be published the next year or in an additional monograph in the same year. Manuscripts are accepted any time of the year.